Unit Resource Guide
Unit 19

Multiplication and Division Problems

THIRD EDITION

KENDALL/HUNT PUBLISHING COMPANY
4050 Westmark Drive   Dubuque, Iowa   52002

A TIMS® Curriculum
University of Illinois at Chicago

UIC The University of Illinois
at Chicago

The original edition was based on work supported by the National Science Foundation under grant No. MDR 9050226 and the University of Illinois at Chicago. Any opinions, findings, and conclusions or recommendations expressed in this publication are those of the author(s) and do not necessarily reflect the views of the granting agencies.

Letter Home

Multiplication and Division Problems

Date: _____

Dear Family Member:

In this unit, we return to the study of multiplication and division. Students solve problems involving multiplying two-digit by one-digit numbers, for example, 73×5. They also extend their division skills.

In the previous multiplication units, students developed their understanding of *what* multiplication is and *when* to use it to solve a problem. Here, our focus is on *how* to multiply. There are three important types of computing: mental, calculator, and paper and pencil. This unit introduces a paper-and-pencil method.

The method for multiplying taught here is different from the traditional one. For example, many people solve a problem like 37×4 as shown:

$$
\begin{array}{r}
2 \\
37 \\
\times\ 4 \\
\hline
148
\end{array}
$$

In the method we use, every product is written down:

$$
\begin{array}{r}
37 \\
\times\ 4 \\
\hline
28 \\
+\ 120 \\
\hline
148
\end{array}
$$

37 ⟶ Think "30 + 7" Step 1

28 ⟵ Multiply 4×7 Step 2

+ 120 ⟵ Multiply 4×30 Step 3

148 ⟵ Add $28 + 120$ Step 4

By showing each step, students further develop their understanding of the multiplication process.

Help your child at home:

- Talk about problems that come up in everyday life, for example, "If gas costs $2.50 per gallon, how much will 5 gallons cost?" or "If eggs cost $1.69 a dozen, about how much will one egg cost?"

- Help your child prepare for a quiz on the last six multiplication facts (4×6, 4×7, 4×8, 6×7, 6×8, 7×8) by reviewing with the *Triangle Flash Cards*.

Thank you for your continued support of your child's learning.

Sincerely,

_____

Carta al hogar

Problemas de multiplicación y división

Fecha: _____

Estimado miembro de familia:

En esta unidad, regresamos al estudio de la multiplicación y la división. Los estudiantes resuelven problemas de multiplicación que requieren multiplicar números de dos dígitos por números de un dígito, por ejemplo, 73 3 5. También aumentan sus habilidades sobre la división.

En las unidades anteriores sobre multiplicación, los estudiantes desarrollaron su comprensión sobre qué es la multiplicación y cuándo puede usarse para resolver un problema. En esta unidad nos concentraremos en cómo multiplicar. Hay tres tipos de cálculo importantes: mental, con calculadora, y con papel y lápiz. Esta unidad presenta un método de papel y lápiz.

El método para multiplicar que se enseña aquí es diferente del método tradicional. Por ejemplo, muchas personas resolverían un problema como 37×4 de la siguiente manera:

$$\begin{array}{r} \overset{2}{37} \\ \times\ 4 \\ \hline 148 \end{array}$$

En el método que usamos nosotros, se escribe cada producto:

37 $\longrightarrow$	Piensa en "30 + 7"	Paso 1
$\times\ 4$		
$\overline{28}$ $\longleftarrow$	Multiplica 4×7	Paso 2
$+\ 120$ $\longleftarrow$	Multiplica 4×30	Paso 3
$\overline{148}$ $\longleftarrow$	Suma $28 + 120$	Paso 4

Al mostrar cada paso, los estudiantes desarrollan aun más su comprensión del proceso de multiplicación.

Ayude a su hijo/a en casa:

• Hablen sobre problemas de la vida cotidiana, por ejemplo, "Si la gasolina cuesta $2.50 por galón, ¿cuánto costarán 5 galones?" o "Si los huevos cuestan $1.69 la docena, ¿cuánto costará un solo huevo aproximadamente?"

• Ayude a su hijo/a a prepararse para un examen sobre las últimas seis multiplicaciones (4×6, 4×7, 4×8, 6×7, 6×8, 7×8) repasándolas con las tarjetas triangulares.

Gracias por su apoyo continuo del aprendizaje de su hijo/a.

Atentamente,

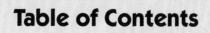

Table of Contents

Unit 19
Multiplication and Division Problems

Unit 19

Outline
Multiplication and Division Problems

Unit Summary

Estimated Class Sessions

9

Students solve multiplication problems by breaking products into the sum of simpler products using rectangular arrays drawn on grid paper. They begin with one-digit by one-digit problems and move to two-digit by one-digit problems. Students write and solve multiplication story problems giving particular attention to partitioning numbers into tens and ones. These problems act as a catalyst for the conceptual development of an algorithm for multiplication involving two-digit by one-digit numbers. In this unit, students also solve division problems that deal with remainders and multistep problems that involve both multiplication and division. The DPP for this unit provides practice with and assesses the last six multiplication facts.

Major Concept Focus

- multiplication strategies
- multiplication stories
- one-digit by two-digit multiplication
- multiplication by multiples of ten
- division strategies
- division stories
- interpreting remainders
- multistep problems
- multiple solution strategies
- practice and assessment of the last six multiplication facts

Assessment Indicators

Use the following Assessment Indicators and the *Observational Assessment Record* that follows the Background section in this unit to assess students on key ideas.

A1. Can students represent 2-digit by 1-digit multiplication problems using manipulatives, arrays, and drawings?

A2. Can students solve 2-digit by 1-digit multiplication problems using manipulatives, arrays, and drawings?

A3. Can students multiply numbers with ending zeros?

A4. Can students write number sentences for multiplication and division situations?

A5. Can students create stories for multiplication and division sentences?

A6. Can students solve multiplication and division problems and explain their reasoning?

A7. Can students interpret remainders?

A8. Do students demonstrate fluency with the multiplication facts for the last six facts $(4 \times 6, 4 \times 7, 4 \times 8, 6 \times 7, 6 \times 8, 7 \times 8)$?

Unit Planner

	Lesson Information	Supplies	Copies/Transparencies
Lesson 1 **Break-apart Products** URG Pages 23–38 SG Pages 286–289 DPP A–B HP Part 1 *Estimated Class Sessions* **1**	**Activity** Students solve multiplication problems by breaking products into the sum of simpler products using rectangular arrays drawn on grid paper. They begin with multiplying one-digit numbers and move to multiplying a two-digit number by a one-digit number. **Math Facts** DPP Bit A provides practice with the last six multiplication facts. **Homework** 1. Assign Home Practice Part 1. 2. Assign *Questions 1–20* in the Homework section of the *Student Guide*. 3. Remind students to practice the last six multiplication facts using the *Triangle Flash Cards*.	• crayons or colored pencils • red and green overhead markers	• 5–6 copies of *Centimeter Grid Paper* URG Page 31 per student • 1 table from *Small Multiplication Tables* URG Page 32 per student • 1 copy of *Triangle Flash Cards: The Last Six Facts* URG Page 33 per student, optional • 1 transparency of *Rectangular Arrays* URG Page 30
Lesson 2 **More Multiplication Stories** URG Pages 39–51 SG Pages 290–294 DPP C–J HP Part 2 *Estimated Class Sessions* **4**	**Activity** Students solve problems that involve multiplying two-digit numbers by one-digit numbers, giving particular attention to partitioning numbers into tens and ones. They write stories to represent the multiplication problems and their partitions. This work leads to the conceptual development of a paper-and-pencil algorithm for multiplication. **Math Facts** DPP Bit E and Task H provide practice with the last six multiplication facts. **Homework** 1. Assign Home Practice Part 2. 2. Assign the Homework section in the *Student Guide*. **Assessment** 1. Ask students to solve the problem 4×34 representing their work Tyrone's Way. Record your observations using the *Observational Assessment Record*. 2. Use the homework problems in the *Student Guide* to assess students' understanding of the paper-and-pencil algorithm.		• 1 table from *Small Multiplication Tables* URG Page 32 per student • 1 copy of *Observational Assessment Record* URG Pages 11–12 to be used throughout this unit

	Lesson Information	**Supplies**	**Copies/ Transparencies**

Lesson 3

Making Groups

URG Pages 52–59

DPP K–L
HP Part 3

Estimated Class Sessions

1

Activity
Students consider the number of groups of equal size that they can make from various numbers of objects. The groupings involve dividing numbers between 25 and 50, including many that cannot be solved just by using fact families. Particular attention is given to remainders.

Math Facts
DPP Bit K provides practice with using doubles to solve multiplication problems.

Homework
1. Assign Home Practice Part 3.
2. Ask students to complete a table for 56 like the one they completed in the lesson.

Assessment
1. While students complete a table like the one in the lesson, observe their abilities to write number sentences for division situations and interpret remainders. Record observations on the *Observational Assessment Record*.
2. Use DPP Task L as an assessment.

• 50 connecting cubes per student

• 4–5 copies of *Four-column Data Table* URG Page 58 per student

Lesson 4

Solving Problems with Division

URG Pages 60–70
SG Pages 295–298

DPP M–R
HP Part 4

Estimated Class Sessions

3

Activity
Students solve multiplication and division word problems, including some division word problems that involve remainders. They also solve challenging multistep problems whose solutions use both multiplication and division.

Math Facts
DPP items P and Q provide practice with and assess multiplication facts.

Homework
1. Assign Home Practice Part 4.
2. Assign the homework problems on the *Solving Problems with Division* Activity Pages.

Assessment
1. DPP Bit Q is a quiz on the last six multiplication facts.
2. Assign the *Multiplication and Division* Assessment Blackline Master. Have multiplication tables available for students.
3. Note students' progress solving multiplication and division problems. Transfer appropriate Unit 19 *Observational Assessment Record* observations to students' *Individual Assessment Record Sheets*.

• base-ten pieces, optional
• connecting cubes, optional
• calculators, optional

• 1 table from *Small Multiplication Tables* URG Page 32 per student
• 1 copy of *Multiplication and Division* URG Page 67 per student
• 1 copy of *Individual Assessment Record Sheet* TIG Assessment section per student, previously copied for use throughout the year

Connections

A current list of literature and software connections is available at *www.mathtrailblazers.com*. You can also find information on connections in the *Teacher Implementation Guide* Literature List and Software List sections.

Software Connections

- *Carmen Sandiego's Math Detective* provides practice with math facts, estimation, ordering numbers, and word problems.
- *Ice Cream Truck* develops problem solving, money skills, and arithmetic operations.
- *Kid Pix* or other drawing software allows students to illustrate stories using computers. (Lesson 2)
- *Math Arena* is a collection of math activities that reinforces many math concepts.
- *Mighty Math Calculating Crew* poses short answer questions about number operations and money skills.
- *National Library of Virtual Manipulatives* website (http://matti.usu.edu) allows students to work with manipulatives including rectangle multiplication that models the all-partials algorithm. (Lesson 2)

Teaching All Math Trailblazers Students

Math Trailblazers® lessons are designed for students with a wide range of abilities. The lessons are flexible and do not require significant adaptation for diverse learning styles or academic levels. However, when needed, lessons can be tailored to allow students to engage their abilities to the greatest extent possible while building knowledge and skills.

To assist you in meeting the needs of all students in your classroom, this section contains information about some of the features in the curriculum that allow all students access to mathematics. For additional information, see the Teaching the *Math Trailblazers* Student: Meeting Individual Needs section in the *Teacher Implementation Guide*.

Differentiation Opportunities in this Unit

DPP Challenges

DPP Challenges are items from the Daily Practice and Problems that usually take more than fifteen minutes to complete. These problems are more thought-provoking and can be used to stretch students' problem-solving skills. The following lessons have DPP Challenges in them:

- DPP Challenge F from Lesson 2 *More Multiplication Stories*
- DPP Challenge N from Lesson 4 *Solving Problems with Division*

Extensions

Use extensions to enrich lessons. Many extensions provide opportunities to further involve or challenge students of all abilities. Take a moment to review the extensions prior to beginning this unit. Some extensions may require additional preparation and planning. The following lesson contains an extension:

- Lesson 4 *Solving Problems with Division*

Background
Multiplication and Division Problems

This unit is the last of four multiplication and division units. In it, students solve problems involving multiplication of two-digit by one-digit numbers and division problems that cannot be solved just by using fact families. They solve multiplication problems by breaking products into the sums of simpler products and write stories that represent their arithmetical processes in a meaningful way. This work leads to the conceptual development of a paper-and-pencil algorithm for the multiplication of two-digit by one-digit numbers. Students solve division problems that deal with remainders in various ways and multistep problems that involve both multiplication and division.

Distributive Law of Multiplication over Addition

In Lesson 1 *Break-apart Products,* students solve multiplication problems by breaking products into the sum of simpler products. For example, 7×4 can be broken into $5 \times 4 + 2 \times 4$. The fundamental property that is involved in this process is the **distributive property of multiplication over addition** (although students do not study this formally). This property states that for any numbers *a, b,* and *c,*

$$(a + b) \times c = (a \times c) + (b \times c)$$

To find 7×4 as expressed above, we partition 7 into two parts, $7 = 5 + 2$, and apply the distributive property with $a = 5$, $b = 2$, and $c = 4$.

The unit does not include formal instruction on the distributive property. However, the activities in this unit will help students to develop an informal understanding of this property. This type of informal understanding is very important as it enables students to do many calculations mentally and is the basis for the traditional paper-and-pencil multiplication algorithm.

Division with and without Remainders

This unit introduces no formal algorithm for division. Students are encouraged to use a variety of strategies for solving division problems with and without remainders. Strategies such as repeated subtraction, manipulative models, and calculators are emphasized, but you should allow students to explore others. Students learn paper-and-pencil methods for division in fourth and fifth grades.

Types of Computing

Students should become proficient in all three types of computing: mental, calculator, and paper and pencil. They also should develop a sense of when each method is appropriate. Furthermore, they should be able to make estimations as well as use each method to find exact answers. This unit develops a paper-and-pencil algorithm for multiplication, but students can also practice other types of computing. They can use mental math to make estimates to verify the reasonableness of their answers, and they can use calculators to check their exact answers.

This unit introduces students to the all-partials algorithm for multiplication. This algorithm is different from the compact algorithm in that it allows students to write all partial products. The lesson guide for Lesson 2 *More Multiplication Stories* discusses this algorithm. You can refer to the TIMS Tutor: *Arithmetic* in the *Teacher Implementation Guide* for more information regarding algorithms. Though we focus on the all-partials algorithm, students should not be discouraged from using other correct paper-and-pencil algorithms that make sense to them.

Resources

- Fuson, K.C. "Developing Mathematical Power in Whole Number Operations." In *A Research Companion to Principles and Standards for School Mathematics*. J. Kilpatrick, W.G. Martin, and D. Schifter, eds. National Council of Teachers of Mathematics, Reston, VA, 2003.

- Lampert, M. "Teaching Multiplication." *Journal of Mathematical Behavior*. Volume 5, Norwood, NJ, pages 241–280, 1986.

- National Research Council. "Developing Proficiency with Whole Numbers." In *Adding It Up: Helping Children Learn Mathematics*. J. Kilpatrick, J. Swafford, and B. Findell, eds. National Academy Press, Washington, DC, 2001.

- *Principles and Standards for School Mathematics*. National Council of Teachers of Mathematics, Reston, VA, 2000.

Observational Assessment Record

A1 Can students represent 2-digit by 1-digit multiplication problems using manipulatives, arrays, and drawings?

A2 Can students solve 2-digit by 1-digit multiplication problems using manipulatives, arrays, and drawings?

A3 Can students multiply numbers with ending zeros?

A4 Can students write number sentences for multiplication and division situations?

A5 Can students create stories for multiplication and division sentences?

A6 Can students solve multiplication and division problems and explain their reasoning?

A7 Can students interpret remainders?

A8 Do students demonstrate fluency with the multiplication facts for the last six facts (4×6, 4×7, 4×8, 6×7, 6×8, 7×8)?

A9 _____

Name	A1	A2	A3	A4	A5	A6	A7	A8	A9	Comments
1.										
2.										
3.										
4.										
5.										
6.										
7.										
8.										
9.										
10.										
11.										
12.										

Name	A1	A2	A3	A4	A5	A6	A7	A8	A9	Comments
13.										
14.										
15.										
16.										
17.										
18.										
19.										
20.										
21.										
22.										
23.										
24.										
25.										
26.										
27.										
28.										
29.										
30.										
31.										
32.										

Unit 19

Daily Practice and Problems
Multiplication and Division Problems

A DPP Menu for Unit 19

Two Daily Practice and Problems (DPP) items are included for each class session listed in the Unit Outline. A scope and sequence chart for the DPP is in the *Teacher Implementation Guide*.

Icons in the Teacher Notes column designate the subject matter of each DPP item. The first item in each class session is always a Bit and the second is either a Task or Challenge. Each item falls into one or more of the categories listed below. A menu of the DPP items for Unit 19 follows.

N Number Sense	✕ Computation	🕐 Time	△ Geometry
D, F–I, K, P	C, D, F–I, L, N, O, R	M	B, J, P

⁵⁄ₓ₇ Math Facts	$ Money	🎚 Measurement	▧ Data
A, E, H, K, P, Q	C, F, I, R	B	

Practicing and Assessing the Multiplication Facts

In Unit 11, students began the systematic, strategies-based study of the multiplication facts. In Unit 19, students review and practice the multiplication facts for the last six facts: $4 \times 6, 4 \times 7, 4 \times 8, 6 \times 7, 6 \times 8, 7 \times 8$. The *Triangle Flash Cards* for these groups were distributed in Unit 15 in the *Discovery Assignment Book* immediately following the Home Practice. They can also be found in Lesson 1. In Unit 19, DPP items A, E, H, K, and P provide practice with multiplication facts for these groups. Bit Q is the Multiplication Quiz: The Last Six Facts. Students will take an inventory test on all the facts in Unit 20.

For information on the distribution and study of the multiplication facts in Grade 3, see the DPP Guide for Units 3 and 11. For a detailed explanation of our approach to learning and assessing the math facts in Grade 3 see the *Grade 3 Facts Resource Guide* and for information for Grades K–5, see the TIMS Tutor: *Math Facts* in the *Teacher Implementation Guide*.

Daily Practice and Problems

Students may solve the items individually, in groups, or as a class. The items may also be assigned for homework. The DPPs are also available on the Teacher Resource CD.

Student Questions	Teacher Notes

(A) Facts: The Last Six Facts

A. $4 \times 8 =$

B. $4 \times 7 =$

C. $7 \times 6 =$

D. $4 \times 6 =$

E. $8 \times 6 =$

F. $8 \times 7 =$

Explain your strategy for Question C.

TIMS Bit

Discuss strategies students use to solve the facts, emphasizing those that are more efficient than others. For example, to solve 7×6, students might double the answer to 7×3. Similarly, students may use doubling to solve facts for 4s. For example, to solve 4×6, students might double 6 to get 12 and then double 12 to get 24. Using break-apart facts is a possible strategy, but may not be efficient for some—$8 \times 7 = 8 \times 5 + 8 \times 2$ or $40 + 16 = 56$. Students may also say, "I just know it." Recall is obviously an efficient strategy.

Students should take home the *Triangle Flash Cards: The Last Six Facts* to study at home with a family member. Tell students when the quiz on this group of facts will be given. DPP Bit Q is Multiplication Quiz: The Last Six Facts.

B Cube Model Plans

Use the cube model plan below to find the following:

1. volume of the model

2. height of the model

3. area of floor

You may build the cube model with connecting cubes if it helps.

Back

5	3	3
4	2	1

Left   Right

Front

TIMS Task

Be sure students use appropriate units when expressing their answers.

1. 18 cubic units

2. 5 units

3. 6 square units

C Adding and Subtracting Money

Complete the following problems. Use pencil and paper or mental math to find the answers.

1. $2.45 − $1.05 =

2. $7.60 + $9.95 =

3. $6.75 − $ .32 =

4. $5.99 + $4.25 =

5. Explain a way to solve Question 4 using mental math.

TIMS Bit

1. $1.40

2. $17.55

3. $6.43

4. $10.24

5. Possible strategy: students may replace $5.99 with $6 and easily add the $4.25. Then they could subtract the last penny for an answer of $10.24.

D Multiplication Story

Write a story and draw a picture about $8 \times \frac{1}{4}$.

Write a number sentence for your picture.

TIMS Task $\boxed{N}$ ✖

Students can share their stories with the class.

E Multiplication Table

Fill in the missing information on this multiplication table.

×	4	6	7	8
4				
6				
7				
8				

TIMS Bit $\boxed{\frac{5}{x\,7}}$

Discuss the strategies students used to complete the multiplication chart. Focus attention on how students solved the last six facts. (4×8, 4×7, 4×6, 7×6, 8×6, and 8×7)

F Making Change

Beth asked for her allowance of $1.70 in nickels and dimes. Her parents gave her $1.00 using one kind of coin and $.70 using the other coin.

1. How many nickels did Beth possibly get? How many dimes?

2. Beth said, "I wanted the same number of nickels as dimes." Is this possible? If so, how many nickels? How many dimes? If not, why?

TIMS Challenge N ❋ $

1. 20 nickels and 7 dimes or 10 dimes and 14 nickels

2. No; 10 nickels is $.50 and 10 dimes is $1.00: $1.50

   12 nickels is $.60 and 12 dimes is $1.20: $1.80

   11 nickels is $.55 and 11 dimes is $1.10: $1.65

G Using Doubles

Solve these problems in your head. Write only the answers. Be ready to explain your answers.

1. $7 + 7 =$ 2. $7 + 6 =$

3. $8 + 7 =$ 4. $80 + 80 =$

5. $90 + 80 =$ 6. $80 + 85 =$

7. $30 + 30 =$ 8. $30 + 32 =$

9. $30 + 25 =$

TIMS Bit ❋ N

1. 14   2. 13
3. 15   4. 160
5. 170   6. 165
7. 60   8. 62
9. 55

These problems are grouped together to encourage students to use doubles to find the answers. For example, $80 + 85$ can be solved by doubling 80 and adding 5 ($80 + 80 + 5$).

H Skip Counting

1. Skip count by 4s to 100. Say the numbers quietly to yourself. Write the numbers.

2. Skip count by 8s until you pass 100. Say the numbers quietly to yourself. Write the numbers.

3. Circle the numbers in your lists that are products of (answers to) the last six facts:

   4×6 4×7 4×8

   6×7 6×8 7×8

4. How could you use skip counting to find these facts?

5. Which of the last six facts is not circled? Why not?

TIMS Task

1–2. If your calculator has the constant feature, press $4 + 4 = = = = = = = =$. Each time $=$ is pressed, the constant number (4) and the constant operation (addition) is repeated. Some students may find it helpful to count by twos, accentuating every other number: 2, <u>4</u>, 6, <u>8</u>, 10, <u>12</u>, 14, <u>16</u>, etc. Then, count by 8s.

Have students write down the numbers as they count. Discuss patterns in the two lists.

3. Students circle 24, 28, 32, 48, and 56 in both lists.

4. Answers will vary. To find 4×8, students can skip count by 4, eight times: 4, 8, 12, 16, 24, 28, (32.)

5. $6 \times 7 = 42$; 42 is not a multiple of 4.

I Lizardland

Use the picture of Lizardland from Unit 11 in your *Student Guide*.

1. Sam wants 2 hot dogs. What will they cost?

2. Sam agrees to treat Adam to 2 hot dogs. How much will 4 hot dogs cost?

3. Tim spent $12 trying to win the Lizard stuffed animal. How many hot dogs could he have bought with the $12?

TIMS Bit

Discuss patterns in these problems. How can doubling help? Discuss strategies used to solve the problems. The sign for Lizard Lunch in the picture of Lizardland shows that one hot dog costs $1.50.

1. $3.00

2. $6.00

3. 8 hot dogs

J Squares and Rectangles

1. Draw a square. Then write what a square is.

2. Draw a rectangle. Then write what a rectangle is.

3. What is the difference between squares and rectangles?

4. Is a square a rectangle?

5. Is a rectangle a square?

TIMS Task

1. A square is a four-sided figure with four right angles and four equal sides. It is a special kind of rectangle.

2. A rectangle is a four-sided figure with four right angles. Opposite sides are parallel and the same length.

3. Students should identify the similarities between the square and the rectangle, such as both have four sides and right angles, and opposite sides are the same length. The only difference is that a square's four sides are all the same length.

4. Yes

5. Not always

K Double, Double Again

Solve these problems.

1. $6 \times 2 =$ 2. $6 \times 4 =$

3. $8 \times 2 =$ 4. $8 \times 4 =$

5. $7 \times 2 =$ 6. $14 \times 2 =$

7. $7 \times 4 =$ 8. $14 \times 4 =$

9. $7 \times 8 =$

TIMS Bit

The first four are from students' multiplication tables. Discuss the patterns and answers before assigning Questions 5–9.

1. 12   2. 24
3. 16   4. 32
5. 14   6. 28
7. 28   8. 56
9. 56

Student Questions	Teacher Notes

L **Multiplication Story**

Solve 38 × 4. Write a story and draw a picture to match your solution.

TIMS Task

152

Stories and pictures will vary.

M **Today, Tonight, or Tomorrow?**

1. What time will it be 4 hours from now?

2. What time will it be $6\frac{1}{3}$ hours from now?

3. What time will it be 8 hours from now?

4. What time will it be $12\frac{1}{4}$ hours from now?

TIMS Bit

Work with a clock, showing the position of the minute hand as students count.

N **Mathhoppers on the Calculator**

1. A +9 mathhopper starts at 2 and hops 15 times. Estimate where it lands.

2. Where does it land exactly? Tell how you know.

3. How many more hops does it need to reach 200?

TIMS Challenge

1. Accept a wide range of estimates. One possibility is to think of a +10 mathhopper hopping 15 times. The +9 mathhopper will then land around 150.

2. 137; Possible keystrokes: 15 × 9 + 2 =

3. 7 more hops; Students may skip count by 9 on the calculator from 137 to 200. Another possibility is to subtract: 200 − 137 = 63. The mathhopper must hop over 63 more numbers. 63 ÷ 9 = 7 hops

Student Questions	Teacher Notes

◎ Some More Sums

Add 27 to each of these numbers.

65	189	2977

TIMS Bit

Students may use base-ten pieces or paper and pencil to find the answers.

92   216   3004

℗ Rectangles and Products

1. Using *Centimeter Grid Paper,* draw all the rectangles you can make with 32 tiles.

2. Draw all the rectangles you can make with 24 tiles.

TIMS Task

Distribute *Centimeter Grid Paper. Centimeter Grid Paper* is available in Lesson 1. Have students draw rectangles that can be formed using tiles.

1. 4 cm by 8 cm
   2 cm by 16 cm
   1 cm by 32 cm (will not fit on grid paper)

2. 6 cm by 4 cm
   8 cm by 3 cm
   12 cm by 2 cm
   24 cm by 1 cm (will not fit on grid paper)

ⓠ Multiplication Quiz: The Last Six Facts

A. $8 \times 6 =$ B. $6 \times 4 =$

C. $4 \times 7 =$ D. $7 \times 8 =$

E. $6 \times 7 =$ F. $8 \times 4 =$

TIMS Bit

This quiz is on the fifth and final group of multiplication facts, the last six facts. We recommend 1 minute for this quiz. Allow students to change pens or pencils after the time is up and complete the remaining problems in a different color.

After students take the test, have them update their *Multiplication Facts I Know* charts.

R Saturday at Lizardland

Use the Lizardland picture from Unit 11 in your *Student Guide* to solve the following problems.

1. On Saturday, in the first hour, 100 adults and 200 children came to Lizardland. How much was collected in ticket sales?

2. Last Saturday 600 adults and 1000 children came to Lizardland. How much was collected in ticket sales?

3. Fifty-nine members of the Jones family reunion came to Lizardland on Saturday. Forty-four family members were children. Fifteen were adults. How much did they pay to get in?

TIMS Task

The admission sign at the entrance to Lizardland in the *Student Guide* lists the adult price (on Saturday) of $6.00 and the children's price of $3.00.

1. $600 + $600 = $1200

2. $3600 + $3000 = $6600

3. 44 × $3 + 15 × $6 = $222

Lesson 1

Break-apart Products

Lesson Overview

Estimated Class Sessions

1

Students break products, such as 6 × 8, into the sum of simpler products, e.g., 6 × 5 + 6 × 3. To do this, they draw a rectangular array on grid paper to represent a product, divide the array into two smaller arrays that represent easier products, and add the easier products to get their answers. They begin with one-digit by one-digit problems and move to two-digit by one-digit problems. In doing this activity, students develop an understanding of the distributive property of multiplication over addition although they do not study it formally.

Key Content

- Representing multiplication problems using arrays.
- Solving multiplication problems by writing them as the sum of easier problems.
- Writing number sentences for multiplication situations.
- Solving multiplication problems and explaining the reasoning.
- Multiplying numbers with ending zeros.

Math Facts

DPP Bit A provides practice with the last six multiplication facts.

Homework

1. Assign Home Practice Part 1.
2. Assign *Questions 1–20* in the Homework section of the *Student Guide*.
3. Remind students to practice the last six multiplication facts using the *Triangle Flash Cards*.

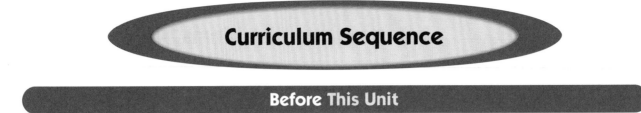

Curriculum Sequence

Multiplication

Students developed multiplication concepts in Grade 3 Units 3, 7, and 11. They began a systematic study of the multiplication facts in Unit 11 and continued the practice and assessment of the multiplication facts in the Daily Practice and Problems in Units 12–19.

Materials List

Supplies and Copies

Student	Teacher
Supplies for Each Student	**Supplies**
• crayons or colored pencils	• red and green overhead markers
Copies	**Copies/Transparencies**
• 5–6 copies of *Centimeter Grid Paper* per student (*Unit Resource Guide* Page 31) • 1 table from *Small Multiplication Tables* per student (*Unit Resource Guide* Page 32) • 1 copy of *Triangle Flash Cards: The Last Six Facts* per student, optional (*Unit Resource Guide* Page 33)	• 1 transparency of *Rectangular Arrays* (*Unit Resource Guide* Page 30)

All blackline masters including assessment, transparency, and DPP masters are also on the Teacher Resource CD.

Student Books

Break-apart Products (*Student Guide* Pages 286–289)

Daily Practice and Problems and Home Practice

DPP items A–B (*Unit Resource Guide* Pages 14–15)
Home Practice Part 1 (*Discovery Assignment Book* Page 268)

Note: Classrooms whose pacing differs significantly from the suggested pacing of the units should use the Math Facts Calendar in Section 4 of the *Facts Resource Guide* to ensure students receive the complete math facts program.

Daily Practice and Problems

Suggestions for using the DPPs are on page 27.

A. Bit: Facts: The Last Six Facts

$\boxed{\begin{smallmatrix} 5 \\ \times\, 7 \end{smallmatrix}}$

(URG p. 14)

A. $4 \times 8 =$ B. $4 \times 7 =$

C. $7 \times 6 =$ D. $4 \times 6 =$

E. $8 \times 6 =$ F. $8 \times 7 =$

Explain your strategy for Question C.

B. Task: Cube Model Plans

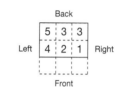

(URG p. 15)

Use the cube model plan below to find the following:

1. volume of the model
2. height of the model
3. area of floor

You may build the cube model with connecting cubes if it helps.

Back

5	3	3
4	2	1

Left   Right

Front

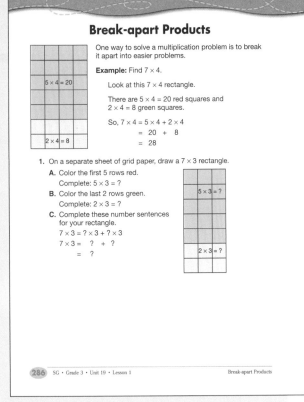

Break-apart Products

One way to solve a multiplication problem is to break it apart into easier problems.

Example: Find 7 × 4.

Look at this 7 × 4 rectangle.

There are 5 × 4 = 20 red squares and 2 × 4 = 8 green squares.

So, 7 × 4 = 5 × 4 + 2 × 4
= 20 + 8
= 28

1. On a separate sheet of grid paper, draw a 7 × 3 rectangle.

   A. Color the first 5 rows red.
      Complete: 5 × 3 = ?
   B. Color the last 2 rows green.
      Complete: 2 × 3 = ?
   C. Complete these number sentences for your rectangle.
      7 × 3 = ? × 3 + ? × 3
      7 × 3 =   ? + ?
            =   ?

286   SG • Grade 3 • Unit 19 • Lesson 1   Break-apart Products

Student Guide - page 286 (Answers on p. 34)

Figure 2: *Rectangle A showing that 7 × 4 = 7 × 2 + 7 × 2*

Teaching the Activity

Show students Rectangle A on the *Rectangular Arrays* Transparency Master. The 7 × 4 rectangle represents the product 7 × 4. Color in the rectangle so that a 5 × 4 rectangle is red and a 2 × 4 rectangle is green, showing that 7 × 4 = 5 × 4 + 2 × 4. Students can follow along with the example in the *Break-apart Products* Activity Pages in the *Student Guide* (See Figure 1). Use the following discussion prompts:

- *How many square centimeters are in this rectangle?* (7 × 4 = 28 sq cm)

- *How many square centimeters are in the red and green regions?* (5 × 4 = 20 sq cm and 2 × 4 = 8 sq cm)

- *This picture shows a way to solve 7 × 4. What is a number sentence that describes that way?* (7 × 4 = 5 × 4 + 2 × 4)

5 × 4 = 20

2 × 4 = 8

Figure 1: *Rectangle A showing that 7 × 4 = 5 × 4 + 2 × 4*

Another way to solve 7 × 4, illustrated in Figure 2, is to break apart the 4 into 2 + 2. You can wipe off your shading on the transparency of Rectangle A and illustrate this second way of solving 7 × 4.

7 × 4 = 7 × 2 + 7 × 2
       =   14   +   14
       =   28

Use the rectangles on the *Rectangular Arrays* transparency to discuss ways to solve the following problems:

    A. 7×4
    B. 4×8
    C. 12×9
    D. 17×3

Encourage students to break apart the products in ways that provide easier products. The example in Figure 1 involves a multiple of 5, which is probably easier for most students than the original multiple of 7. On the other hand, breaking 7×4 into $3 \times 4 + 4 \times 4$ might not be much easier.

Products that have at least one factor between 10 and 20, such as problems C and D, can be broken apart so that one of the easier products involves 10. For D, students can break apart the product in this way: $17 \times 3 = 10 \times 3 + 7 \times 3$. Again, point out that it is helpful to break numbers into products that are easier. Breaking 17×3 into $13 \times 3 + 4 \times 3$ is correct, but probably not any easier to solve.

After working together to break apart several products, ask students to solve *Questions 1–6* on the *Break-apart Products* Activity Pages. They will use grid paper for all the in-class problems.

Breaking apart products allows students to do many calculations mentally and is, in fact, the basis for the traditional paper-and-pencil multiplication algorithm. The fundamental property that is involved in breaking apart products is the distributive property of multiplication over addition. (See the Background section of this unit.) Informal understanding of this property is very important for students; however, formal study at this stage is not necessary.

Math Facts

DPP Bit A provides practice with the last six multiplication facts in preparation for the quiz in this unit.

Homework and Practice

- DPP Task B asks students to use a cube model plan to find the area, volume, and height of a three-dimensional shape.

- Remind students to take home their *Triangle Flash Cards: The Last Six Facts* to prepare for the quiz in DPP Bit Q.

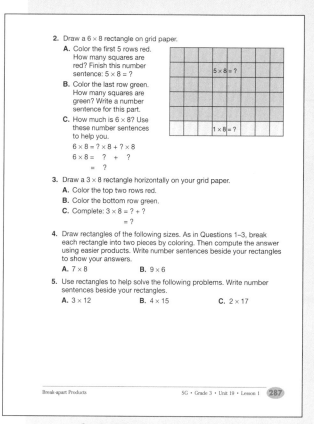

Student Guide - page 287 *(Answers on p. 35)*

2. Draw a 6×8 rectangle on grid paper.
   A. Color the first 5 rows red. How many squares are red? Finish this number sentence: $5 \times 8 = ?$
   B. Color the last row green. How many squares are green? Write a number sentence for this part.
   C. How much is 6×8? Use these number sentences to help you.
      $6 \times 8 = ? \times 8 + ? \times 8$
      $6 \times 8 = \ ? \ + \ ?$
      $\quad\quad = \ ?$

3. Draw a 3×8 rectangle horizontally on your grid paper.
   A. Color the top two rows red.
   B. Color the bottom row green.
   C. Complete: $3 \times 8 = ? + ?$
         $\quad\quad\quad\ = ?$

4. Draw rectangles of the following sizes. As in Questions 1–3, break each rectangle into two pieces by coloring. Then compute the answer using easier products. Write number sentences beside your rectangles to show your answers.
   A. 7×8 B. 9×6

5. Use rectangles to help solve the following problems. Write number sentences beside your rectangles.
   A. 3×12 B. 4×15 C. 2×17

Break-apart Products   SG • Grade 3 • Unit 19 • Lesson 1   **287**

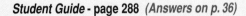
Student Guide - page 288 (Answers on p. 36)

Student Guide - page 289 (Answers on p. 37)

• Students will need two or three copies of *Centimeter Grid Paper* to solve the problems in the Homework section of the *Student Guide*. Homework *Questions 1–8* provide more examples of two-digit by one-digit multiplication. *Questions 9–20* provide practice with multiplication by tens which will be helpful for the next lesson. Have students take home a *Small Multiplication Table* to help them find needed multiplication facts. *Questions 1* and *2* of the Homework section present an opportunity to discuss solutions that are more efficient than others.

• Home Practice Part 1 asks students to estimate sums using benchmarks.

Answers for Part 1 of the Home Practice are in the Answer Key at the end of this lesson and at the end of this unit.

Assessment

Use *Questions 3–6* in the Homework section to assess students' abilities to represent and solve 2-digit by 1-digit multiplication problems using drawings. Students will need two copies of *Centimeter Grid Paper*. Use *Questions 9–20* of the Homework section to assess students' abilities to multiply numbers with ending zeros.

Discovery Assignment Book - page 268 (Answers on p. 38)

At a Glance

Math Facts and Daily Practice and Problems

DPP Bit A provides practice with the last six multiplication facts. Task B asks students to find volume, floor area, and height of a three-dimensional shape.

Teaching the Activity

1. Color Rectangle A on the *Rectangular Arrays* transparency to find the product 7 × 4. Then do it a second way.
2. Discuss different ways to solve problems A–D on the transparency by coloring rectangular arrays.
3. Students use grid paper to solve *Questions 1–6* from the *Break-apart Products* Activity Pages.

Homework

1. Assign Home Practice Part 1.
2. Assign *Questions 1–20* in the Homework section of the *Student Guide.*
3. Remind students to practice the last six multiplication facts using the *Triangle Flash Cards.*

Assessment

Use homework *Questions 3–6* and *Questions 9–20* to assess students on multiplication.

Answer Key is on pages 34–38.

Notes:

Rectangular Arrays

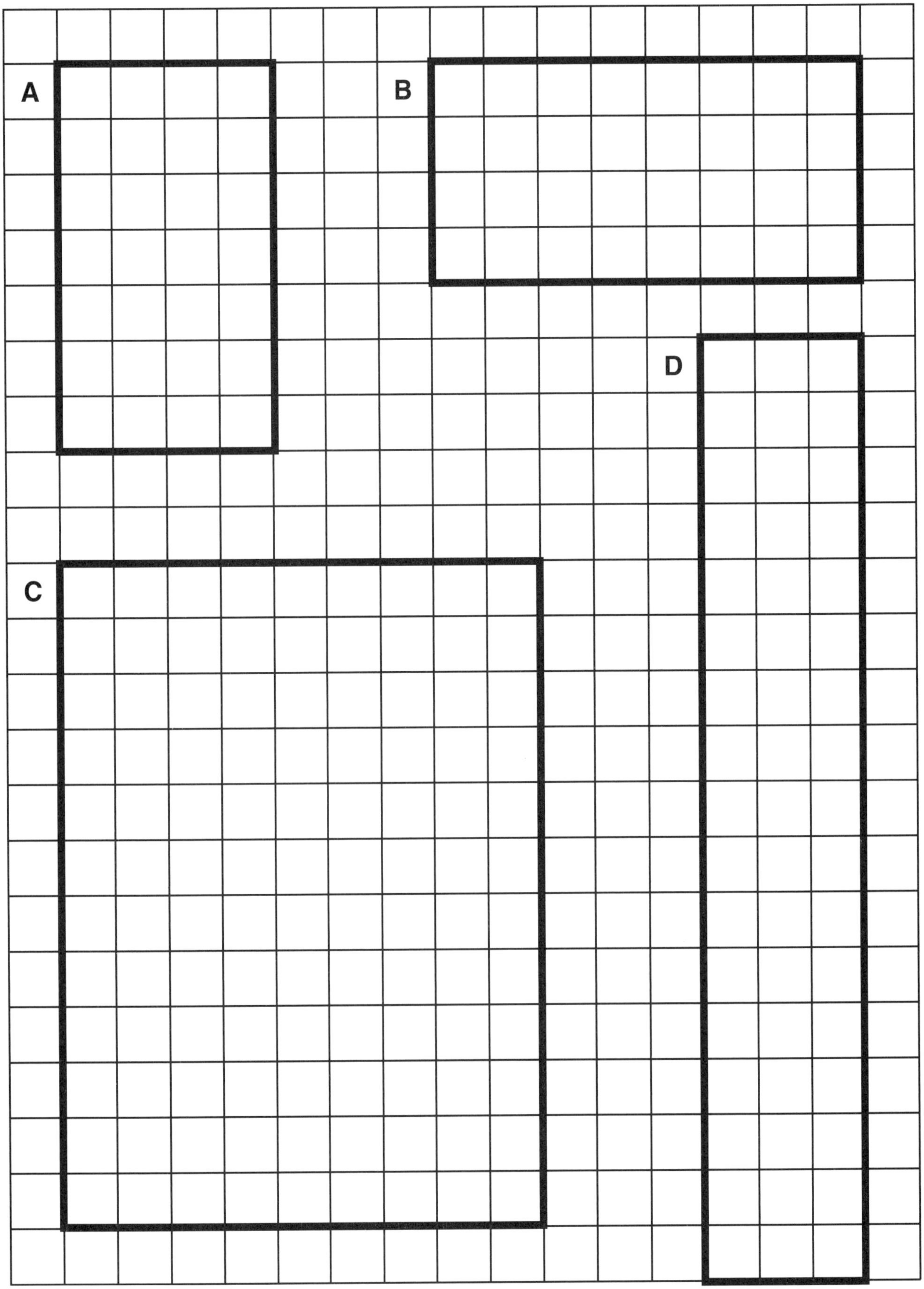

A

B

D

C

Transparency Master

Name _____   Date _____

Centimeter Grid Paper

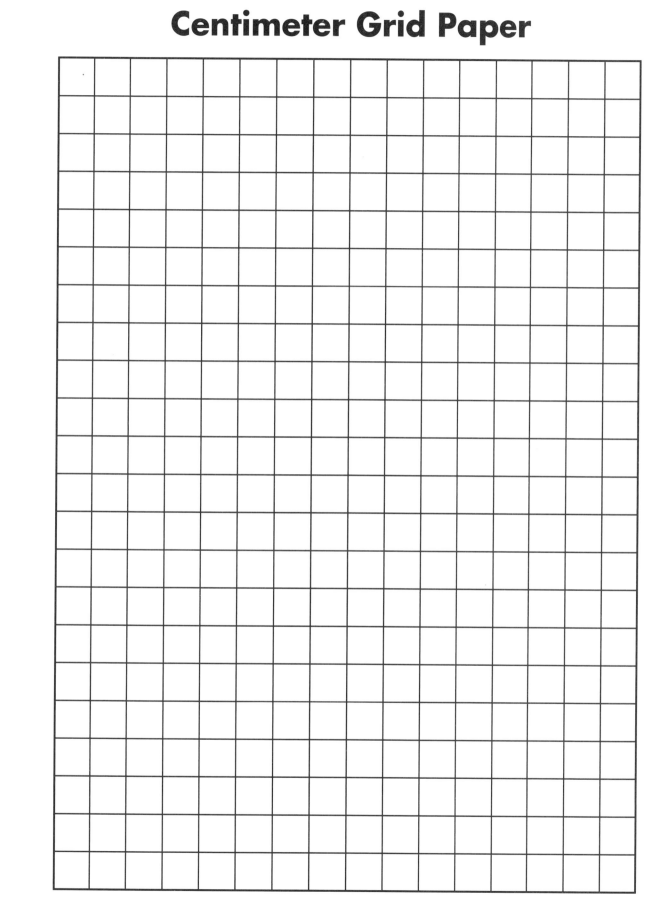

Small Multiplication Tables

×	0	1	2	3	4	5	6	7	8	9	10
0	0	0	0	0	0	0	0	0	0	0	0
1	0	1	2	3	4	5	6	7	8	9	10
2	0	2	4	6	8	10	12	14	16	18	20
3	0	3	6	9	12	15	18	21	24	27	30
4	0	4	8	12	16	20	24	28	32	36	40
5	0	5	10	15	20	25	30	35	40	45	50
6	0	6	12	18	24	30	36	42	48	54	60
7	0	7	14	21	28	35	42	49	56	63	70
8	0	8	16	24	32	40	48	56	64	72	80
9	0	9	18	27	36	45	54	63	72	81	90
10	0	10	20	30	40	50	60	70	80	90	100

×	0	1	2	3	4	5	6	7	8	9	10
0	0	0	0	0	0	0	0	0	0	0	0
1	0	1	2	3	4	5	6	7	8	9	10
2	0	2	4	6	8	10	12	14	16	18	20
3	0	3	6	9	12	15	18	21	24	27	30
4	0	4	8	12	16	20	24	28	32	36	40
5	0	5	10	15	20	25	30	35	40	45	50
6	0	6	12	18	24	30	36	42	48	54	60
7	0	7	14	21	28	35	42	49	56	63	70
8	0	8	16	24	32	40	48	56	64	72	80
9	0	9	18	27	36	45	54	63	72	81	90
10	0	10	20	30	40	50	60	70	80	90	100

×	0	1	2	3	4	5	6	7	8	9	10
0	0	0	0	0	0	0	0	0	0	0	0
1	0	1	2	3	4	5	6	7	8	9	10
2	0	2	4	6	8	10	12	14	16	18	20
3	0	3	6	9	12	15	18	21	24	27	30
4	0	4	8	12	16	20	24	28	32	36	40
5	0	5	10	15	20	25	30	35	40	45	50
6	0	6	12	18	24	30	36	42	48	54	60
7	0	7	14	21	28	35	42	49	56	63	70
8	0	8	16	24	32	40	48	56	64	72	80
9	0	9	18	27	36	45	54	63	72	81	90
10	0	10	20	30	40	50	60	70	80	90	100

×	0	1	2	3	4	5	6	7	8	9	10
0	0	0	0	0	0	0	0	0	0	0	0
1	0	1	2	3	4	5	6	7	8	9	10
2	0	2	4	6	8	10	12	14	16	18	20
3	0	3	6	9	12	15	18	21	24	27	30
4	0	4	8	12	16	20	24	28	32	36	40
5	0	5	10	15	20	25	30	35	40	45	50
6	0	6	12	18	24	30	36	42	48	54	60
7	0	7	14	21	28	35	42	49	56	63	70
8	0	8	16	24	32	40	48	56	64	72	80
9	0	9	18	27	36	45	54	63	72	81	90
10	0	10	20	30	40	50	60	70	80	90	100

Name _____   Date _____

Triangle Flash Cards:
The Last Six Facts

- Work with a partner. Each partner cuts out the 6 flash cards.

- Your partner chooses one card at a time and covers the shaded number. Multiply the two uncovered numbers.

- Divide the used cards into three piles: those you know and can answer quickly, those you can figure out, and those you need to learn.

- Practice the last two piles again. Then make a list of the facts you need to practice at home.

- Repeat the directions for your partner.

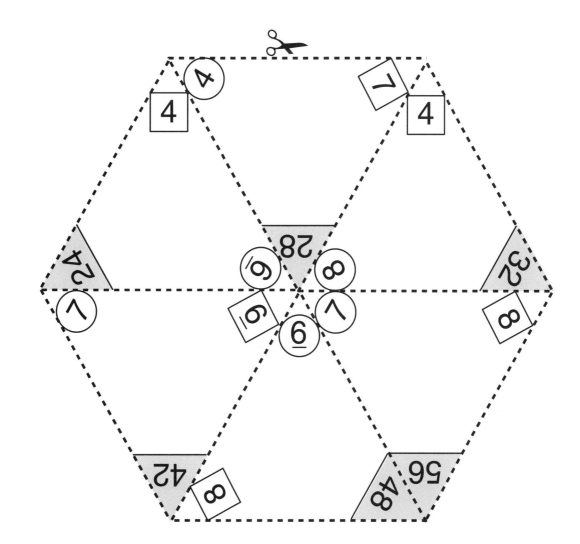

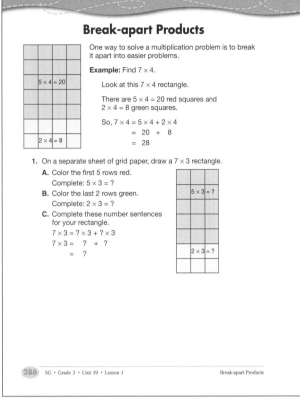

Break-apart Products

One way to solve a multiplication problem is to break it apart into easier problems.

Example: Find 7×4.

Look at this 7×4 rectangle.

There are $5 \times 4 = 20$ red squares and $2 \times 4 = 8$ green squares.

So, $7 \times 4 = 5 \times 4 + 2 \times 4$
$= 20 + 8$
$= 28$

1. On a separate sheet of grid paper, draw a 7×3 rectangle.

   A. Color the first 5 rows red.
   Complete: $5 \times 3 = ?$

   B. Color the last 2 rows green.
   Complete: $2 \times 3 = ?$

   C. Complete these number sentences for your rectangle.
   $7 \times 3 = ? \times 3 + ? \times 3$
   $7 \times 3 = ? + ?$
   $= ?$

Student Guide - page 286

Student Guide (p. 286)

Break-apart Products

I.

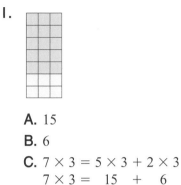

A. 15

B. 6

C. $7 \times 3 = 5 \times 3 + 2 \times 3$
$7 \times 3 = 15 + 6$
$= 21$

Student Guide (p. 287)

2.

A. 40 squares, $5 \times 8 = 40$

B. 8 squares, $1 \times 8 = 8$

C. $6 \times 8 = 5 \times 8 + 1 \times 8$

$6 \times 8 = 40 + 8$

$= 48$

3A.–B.

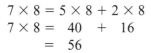

C. $3 \times 8 = 16 + 8 = 24$

4. Solution strategies may vary. One possible strategy is shown for each.

A.

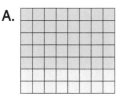

$7 \times 8 = 5 \times 8 + 2 \times 8$

$7 \times 8 = 40 + 16$

$= 56$

B.

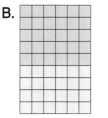

$9 \times 6 = 5 \times 6 + 4 \times 6$

$9 \times 6 = 30 + 24$

$= 54$

5. Solution strategies may vary. One possible strategy is shown.

A.

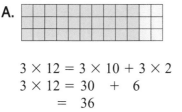

$3 \times 12 = 3 \times 10 + 3 \times 2$

$3 \times 12 = 30 + 6$

$= 36$

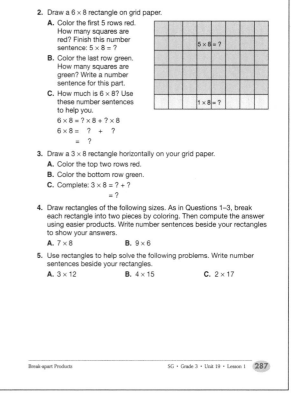

Student Guide - page 287

B.

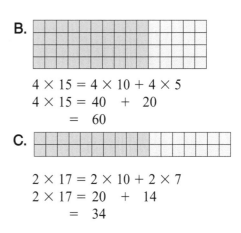

$4 \times 15 = 4 \times 10 + 4 \times 5$

$4 \times 15 = 40 + 20$

$= 60$

C.

$2 \times 17 = 2 \times 10 + 2 \times 7$

$2 \times 17 = 20 + 14$

$= 34$

6. Rachel found 5 × 12 by breaking the 12 apart. One part was a 10.

$5 \times 12 = 5 \times 10 + 5 \times 2$

$= 50 + 10$

$= 60$

Ben found 5 × 12 by breaking the 12 into two equal parts:

$5 \times 12 = 5 \times 6 + 5 \times 6$

$= 30 + 30$

$= 60$

Solve the following problems by breaking them apart. Use Rachel's method at least twice, and use Ben's method at least twice.

A. 5 × 18 = ? **B.** 16 × 3 = ?

C. 6 × 14 = ? **D.** 4 × 23 = ?

E. 13 × 4 = ? **F.** 2 × 36 = ?

(Homework)

You will need *Centimeter Grid Paper* to complete this homework.
Hannah broke apart a rectangle to find 12 × 4. Her solution is shown below.

There are
8 × 4 = 32
green squares
and 4 × 4 = 16
red squares.

8 × 4 = 32   4 × 4 = 16

So, 12 × 4 = 8 × 4 + 4 × 4

$= 32 + 16$

$= 48$

1. Draw a 12 × 4 rectangle on a separate sheet of *Centimeter Grid Paper*. Use this rectangle to show a different method than Hannah's. Write number sentences beside your rectangle to show your answer.

288 SG • Grade 3 • Unit 19 • Lesson 1   Break-apart Products

Student Guide - page 288

Homework

Solution strategies may vary.

1. Possible answer:

$12 \times 4 = 10 \times 4 + 2 \times 4$

$12 \times 4 = 40 + 8$

$= 48$

Student Guide (p. 288)

6. Using Rachel's method:

A. $5 \times 18 = 5 \times 10 + 5 \times 8$

$5 \times 18 = 50 + 40$

$= 90$

B. $16 \times 3 = 10 \times 3 + 6 \times 3$

$16 \times 3 = 30 + 18$

$= 48$

C. $6 \times 14 = 6 \times 10 + 6 \times 4$

$6 \times 14 = 60 + 24$

$= 84$

D. $4 \times 23 = 4 \times 20 + 4 \times 3$

$4 \times 23 = 80 + 12$

$= 92$

E. $13 \times 4 = 10 \times 4 + 3 \times 4$

$13 \times 4 = 40 + 12$

$= 52$

F. $2 \times 36 = 2 \times 30 + 2 \times 6$

$2 \times 36 = 60 + 12$

$= 72$

Using Ben's method:

A. $5 \times 18 = 5 \times 9 + 5 \times 9$

$5 \times 18 = 45 + 45$

$= 90$

B. $16 \times 3 = 8 \times 3 + 8 \times 3$

$16 \times 3 = 24 + 24$

$= 48$

C. $6 \times 14 = 6 \times 7 + 6 \times 7$

$6 \times 14 = 42 + 42$

$= 84$

D. $4 \times 23 = 2 \times 23 + 2 \times 23$

$4 \times 23 = 46 + 46$

$= 92$

E. $13 \times 4 = 13 \times 2 + 13 \times 2$

$13 \times 4 = 26 + 26$

$= 52$

F. $2 \times 36 = 2 \times 18 + 2 \times 18$

$2 \times 36 = 36 + 36$

$= 72$

*Answers and/or discussion are included in the Lesson Guide.

Student Guide (p. 289)

2. Answers may vary. Possible solutions

$14 \times 4 = 10 \times 4 + 4 \times 4$
$14 \times 4 = \quad 40 \quad + \quad 16$
$\quad = \quad 56$

$14 \times 4 = 14 \times 2 + 14 \times 2$
$\quad = \quad 28 \quad + \quad 28$
$\quad = \quad 56$

3. $5 \times 12 = 5 \times 6 + 5 \times 6$
$5 \times 12 = \quad 30 \quad + \quad 30$
$\quad = \quad 60$

4. $2 \times 15 = 2 \times 10 + 2 \times 5$
$2 \times 15 = \quad 20 \quad + \quad 10$
$\quad = \quad 30$

5. $5 \times 24 = 5 \times 20 + 5 \times 4$
$5 \times 24 = \quad 100 \quad + \quad 20$
$\quad = \quad 120$

6. $14 \times 3 = 10 \times 3 + 4 \times 3$
$14 \times 3 = \quad 30 \quad + \quad 12$
$\quad = \quad 42$

7. $9 \times 6 = 9 \times 3 + 9 \times 3$
$9 \times 6 = \quad 27 \quad + \quad 27$
$\quad = \quad 54$

8. $3 \times 13 = 3 \times 10 + 3 \times 3$
$3 \times 13 = \quad 30 \quad + \quad 9$
$\quad = \quad 39$

9. 40
10. 140
11. 180
12. 350
13. 270
14. 160
15. 160
16. 480
17. 630
18. 400
19. 360
20. 150

2. Draw two 14 × 4 rectangles on a sheet of *Centimeter Grid Paper.* Find 14 × 4 by breaking the rectangles apart. Show two different methods. Write number sentences beside your rectangles to show your answers.

Find the following products by breaking them apart into simpler products. Use *Centimeter Grid Paper* to help you.

3. 5×12 4. 2×15 5. 5×24
6. 14×3 7. 9×6 8. 3×13

Review

Find the following products any way you like. You do not have to use the break-apart method. You may use your multiplication table to help you.

9. 10×4 10. 7×20
11. 3×60 12. 5×70
13. 9×30 14. 8×20
15. 4×40 16. 6×80
17. 7×90 18. 5×80
19. 9×40 20. 3×50

Break-apart Products   SG • Grade 3 • Unit 19 • Lesson 1   289

Student Guide - page 289

*Answers and/or discussion are included in the Lesson Guide.

Name _____ Date _____

Unit 19 Home Practice

PART 1

Tell whether the sum of each is more than 600, less than 600, or equal to 600.

1. 300 + 300 _____
2. 318 + 264 _____
3. 268 + 295 _____
4. 329 + 282 _____
5. 240 + 360 _____
6. 363 + 302 _____

Fill in the blanks below so each number sentence equals 1000.

7. ____ + ____ + 300 = 1000
8. ____ + 150 + ____ = 1000
9. 335 + ____ + ____ = 1000

PART 2

1.	2.	3.	4.	5.	6.
79 +69	979 −430	75 × 4	32 × 9	60 × 4	83 × 7

7. Find two 3-digit numbers whose sum is 251. _____
_____

8. Find two numbers whose difference is 79. _____
_____

268 DAB • Grade 3 • Unit 19   MULTIPLICATION AND DIVISION PROBLEMS

Discovery Assignment Book - page 268

Discovery Assignment Book (p. 268)

Home Practice*

Part 1

1. equal
2. less than
3. less than
4. more than
5. equal
6. more than
7. Answers will vary. One example is
$400 + 300 + 300 = 1000$
8. Answers will vary. One example is
$350 + 150 + 500 = 1000$
9. Answers will vary. One example is
$335 + 165 + 500 = 1000$

*Answers for all the Home Practice in the *Discovery Assignment Book* are at the end of the unit.

Lesson 2

More Multiplication Stories

Estimated Class Sessions
4

Students solve two-digit by one-digit multiplication problems. After exploring and discussing their own methods of solving these problems, students focus on the method of breaking apart products into the sum of simpler products. They pay particular attention to partitioning numbers into tens and ones. They then write stories to represent the multiplication problems and refine the stories to reflect their partitions. This work leads to the development of a paper-and-pencil algorithm.

Key Content
- Breaking products into the sum of simpler products (applying the distributive law of multiplication over addition).
- Creating stories for multiplication situations.
- Solving 2-digit by 1-digit multiplication problems using drawings and paper and pencil.

Key Vocabulary
- partition

Math Facts
DPP Bit E and Task H provide practice with the last six multiplication facts.

Homework
1. Assign Home Practice Part 2.
2. Assign the Homework section in the *Student Guide*.

Assessment
1. Ask students to solve the problem 4 × 34 representing their work Tyrone's Way. Record your observations using the *Observational Assessment Record*.
2. Use the homework problems in the *Student Guide* to assess students' understanding of the paper-and-pencil algorithm.

Curriculum Sequence

Before This Unit

Multiplication Stories

Students wrote multiplication stories and drew pictures for single-digit multiplication problems in Grade 3 Unit 3 Lesson 3.

Materials List

Supplies and Copies

Student	Teacher
Supplies for Each Student	**Supplies**
Copies • 1 table from *Small Multiplication Tables* per student (*Unit Resource Guide* Page 32)	**Copies/Transparencies** • 1 copy of *Observational Assessment Record* to be used throughout this unit (*Unit Resource Guide* Pages 11–12)

All blackline masters including assessment, transparency, and DPP masters are also on the Teacher Resource CD.

Student Books
More Multiplication Stories (*Student Guide* Pages 290–294)

Daily Practice and Problems and Home Practice
DPP items C–J (*Unit Resource Guide* Pages 15–19)
Home Practice Part 2 (*Discovery Assignment Book* Page 268)

Note: Classrooms whose pacing differs significantly from the suggested pacing of the units should use the Math Facts Calendar in Section 4 of the *Facts Resource Guide* to ensure students receive the complete math facts program.

Assessment Tools
Observational Assessment Record (*Unit Resource Guide* Pages 11–12)

Daily Practice and Problems

Suggestions for using the DPPs are on page 47.

C. Bit: Adding and Subtracting Money (URG p. 15)

Complete the following problems. Use pencil and paper or mental math to find the answers.

1. $2.45 − $1.05 =
2. $7.60 + $9.95 =
3. $6.75 − $ .32 =
4. $5.99 + $4.25 =
5. Explain a way to solve Question 4 using mental math.

F. Challenge: Making Change (URG p. 17)

Beth asked for her allowance of $1.70 in nickels and dimes. Her parents gave her $1.00 using one kind of coin and $.70 using the other coin.

1. How many nickels did Beth possibly get? How many dimes?
2. Beth said, "I wanted the same number of nickels as dimes." Is this possible? If so, how many nickels? How many dimes? If not, why?

D. Task: Multiplication Story (URG p. 16)

Write a story and draw a picture about $8 \times \frac{1}{4}$.

Write a number sentence for your picture.

G. Bit: Using Doubles (URG p. 17)

Solve these problems in your head. Write only the answers. Be ready to explain your answers.

1. 7 + 7 =
2. 7 + 6 =
3. 8 + 7 =
4. 80 + 80 =
5. 90 + 80 =
6. 80 + 85 =
7. 30 + 30 =
8. 30 + 32 =
9. 30 + 25 =

E. Bit: Multiplication Table (URG p. 16)

Fill in the missing information on this multiplication table.

×	4	6	7	8
4				
6				
7				
8				

H. Task: Skip Counting (URG p. 18)

1. Skip count by 4s to 100. Say the numbers quietly to yourself. Write the numbers.
2. Skip count by 8s until you pass 100. Say the numbers quietly to yourself. Write the numbers.
3. Circle the numbers in your lists that are products of (answers to) the last six facts:

    4×6 4×7 4×8

    6×7 6×8 7×8

4. How could you use skip counting to find these facts?
5. Which of the last six facts is not circled? Why not?

Daily Practice and Problems

Suggestions for using the DPPs are on page 47.

I. Bit: Lizardland (URG p. 18) N $ ✖

Use the picture of Lizardland from Unit 11 in your *Student Guide*.

1. Sam wants 2 hot dogs. What will they cost?
2. Sam agrees to treat Adam to 2 hot dogs. How much will 4 hot dogs cost?
3. Tim spent $12 trying to win the Lizard stuffed animal. How many hot dogs could he have bought with the $12?

J. Task: Squares and Rectangles
(URG p. 19)

1. Draw a square. Then write what a square is.
2. Draw a rectangle. Then write what a rectangle is.
3. What is the difference between squares and rectangles?
4. Is a square a rectangle?
5. Is a rectangle a square?

Teaching the Activity

Provide students with copies of the *Small Multiplication Tables* so they can find any facts they need.

Part 1 Writing Multiplication Stories

Students will write stories to represent two-digit by one-digit multiplication problems. To begin, write a one-digit by one-digit multiplication problem on the board, e.g., 4 × 8, and ask the children to write and illustrate a story to represent it. (They did this type of work in the activity *Multiplication Stories* from Unit 3 *Exploring Multiplication* and should be familiar with it.) Here is an example story for 4 × 8:

There were 4 shirts, and each shirt had 8 buttons. The total number of buttons on the shirts was 4 × 8 = 32. (See Figure 3.)

Next, write a one-digit by two-digit problem on the board, e.g., 4 × 26, and ask students to write a story for it. These stories will be similar to the first ones, except for the size of the numbers. Ask students to illustrate their stories and to solve the multiplication problem. Encourage them to think of their own methods. Have children explain their methods to the class. Below are some methods they might use for 4 × 26:

1. 4 × 26 is 26 + 26 + 26 + 26. I'll break apart each 26 to get 20 + 20 + 20 + 20 + 6 + 6 + 6 + 6 = 104.

2. 26 is 25 + 1. I know that 2 × 25 = 50, so I double that to get 4 × 25 = 100. Then, I add 4 × 1 and get 104.

3. If I think about money, 26¢ is 25¢ + 1¢. I know that 4 quarters are $1.00 and that 4 pennies are 4¢. So, 4 × 26¢ is $1.04. That is the same as 104¢, so 4 × 26 = 104.

4. $4 \times 26 = 4 \times 10 + 4 \times 10 + 4 \times 6$
   $= 40 + 40 + 24$
   $= 104$

5. $4 \times 26 = 4 \times 20 + 4 \times 6$
   $= 80 + 24$
   $= 104$

Figure 3: *4 shirts, each with 8 buttons, have 4 × 8 = 32 buttons*

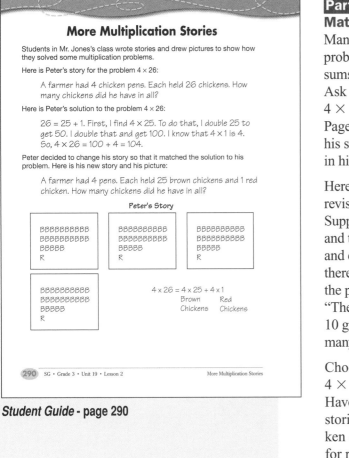

Student Guide - page 290

Student Guide - page 291

Many of the ways students solve their multiplication problems will involve breaking numbers apart into sums of easier products as in methods 2 through 5. Ask students to read Peter's story and solution to 4×26 on the *More Multiplication Stories* Activity Pages in the *Student Guide.* Point out that he revised his story to reflect the way he broke apart the numbers in his solution.

Here is an example of another way a student might revise a story to match a partition used in a solution. Suppose the student used method 4 to solve 4×26 and that his or her story was, "There were 4 packages, and each held 26 popsicles. How many popsicles were there in all?" This story could be revised to match the partitioning of 26 into $10 + 10 + 6$ as follows: "There were 4 boxes. Each held 10 cherry popsicles, 10 grape popsicles, and 6 orange popsicles. How many popsicles were there in all?"

Choose a few solutions that the class wrote for 4×26 and that involve breaking numbers apart. Have the class help revise the corresponding stories so they match the way the numbers were broken apart. Not all the stories will be good candidates for revising this way since they were not written with that goal in mind. When children write multiplication stories later in this activity, suggest they keep revision needs in mind.

Part 3 Breaking Factors into Tens and Ones

After discussing various ways to multiply, tell students you want them to focus at this time on a particular way to break apart products: partitioning factors into tens and ones. This is important practice since this partition is used in the paper-and-pencil multiplication algorithm.

The *More Multiplication Stories* Activity Pages continue with two stories—Libby's story for 72×3 and Alex's story for 63×4—which involve partitioning one factor into tens and ones. Discuss these with the class. Here is another example problem you can use with the class:

6×53. *There were 6 buses, and each had 50 passengers. Then, 3 more passengers got on each bus. How many passengers were there altogether?* $6 \times 50 + 6 \times 3 = 300 + 18 = 318$.

Figure 4: *6 × 53 passengers*

Continue writing and illustrating stories for several more two-digit by one-digit multiplication problems, first as a class and then individually when the students are ready. The stories should have a common theme of splitting groups into smaller groups of tens and ones. These stories should allow children to represent the arithmetic process used to solve multiplication problems in a way that is meaningful to them.

In the past, we have often suggested that students use pictures and manipulatives to help them solve problems. In this case, drawing pictures should help them see why a particular way of solving multiplication problems—breaking apart products into tens and ones—makes sense. Creating a number sentence for their pictures will help students connect the arithmetic process they use to standard symbols.

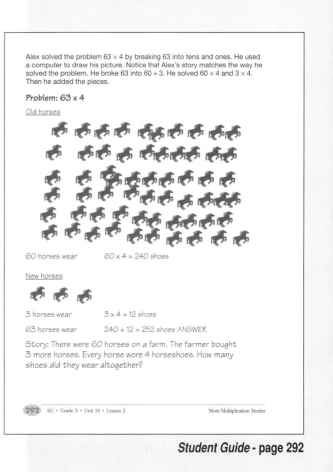

Alex solved the problem 63 × 4 by breaking 63 into tens and ones. He used a computer to draw his picture. Notice that Alex's story matches the way he solved the problem. He broke 63 into 60 + 3. He solved 60 × 4 and 3 × 4. Then he added the pieces.

Problem: 63 x 4

Old horses

60 horses wear   60 x 4 = 240 shoes

New horses

3 horses wear   3 x 4 = 12 shoes
63 horses wear   240 + 12 = 252 shoes ANSWER

Story: There were 60 horses on a farm. The farmer bought 3 more horses. Every horse wore 4 horseshoes. How many shoes did they wear altogether?

292   SG • Grade 3 • Unit 19 • Lesson 2   More Multiplication Stories

Student Guide - page 292

Student Guide - page 293

Student Guide - page 294 *(Answers on p. 50)*

In the Solving Problems Tyrone's Way section on the *More Multiplication Stories* Activity Pages, students are presented with eight two-digit by one-digit multiplication problems to solve. As a means of organizing their work, students are asked to model it in the same way that Tyrone solved 5 × 37. First, they should write the problem at the top of the page. Then, they should divide their solutions into four parts: products to add, calculations, story, and picture. Their answers should be clearly indicated on their work.

Part 4 An Algorithm for Multiplication (Maria's Way)

After students solve many problems, introduce the paper-and-pencil multiplication algorithm shown in the Solving Problems Maria's Way section in the *Student Guide*.

```
  37    ⟶   30 + 7      step 1
×  4
  28    ⟵   4 × 7       step 2
+120    ⟵   4 × 30      step 3
 148              answer
```

This algorithm, called the *all-partials algorithm,* allows students to record all partial products. By having students record all the intermediate products, they should develop a solid understanding of the algorithm. Students practice using this algorithm in *Questions 9–16.*

It is important that students check whether their answers are reasonable after any paper-and-pencil or calculator calculation. Sometimes, computed answers are ridiculously incorrect and a simple mental estimate will catch the error. For example, a child might estimate that the answer to 37 × 4 should be a little less than 160 since 40 × 4 = 160. If he or she had a computed answer of 148, this would be reasonable. Students should develop the important habit of checking whether their answers make sense.

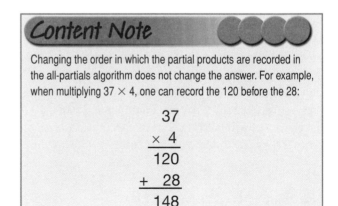

Content Note

Changing the order in which the partial products are recorded in the all-partials algorithm does not change the answer. For example, when multiplying 37 × 4, one can record the 120 before the 28:

```
   37
×   4
  120
+  28
  148
```

Math Facts

DPP Bit E asks students to complete a multiplication table for the last six facts. Task H develops strategies for the last six facts using skip counting.

Homework and Practice

- DPP Bit C provides addition and subtraction practice with money. Task D asks students to draw a picture for a multiplication problem involving a fraction. Items F and I are sets of word problems. Bit G develops mental math skills. Task J asks students to compare rectangles and squares.

- After students work through the problems in the *Student Guide* sections Solving Problems Tyrone's Way and Solving Problems Maria's Way, they can do the Homework section. Have students take home their *Small Multiplication Tables*.

- Home Practice Part 2 provides further practice with addition, subtraction, and multiplication computation.

Answers for Part 2 of the Home Practice are in the Answer Key at the end of this lesson and at the end of this unit.

Assessment

- Ask students to solve the problem 4 × 34 using Tyrone's Way to represent their work. You can use this activity to assess students' abilities to create stories for multiplication sentences and explain their solution strategies. Record your observations using the *Observational Assessment Record*.

- Use the homework problems on the *More Multiplication Stories* Activity Pages to assess students' understanding of the paper-and-pencil algorithm.

Software Connection

- *Kid Pix* or other drawing software.

  If you have access to computers that are equipped with a drawing program, students can use computers to illustrate their multiplication stories. Josh's picture on the *More Multiplication Stories* Activity Pages was drawn using *Kid Pix*.

- *National Library of Virtual Manipulatives* website (http://matti.usu.edu). This website allows students to work with manipulatives including rectangle multiplication that models the all-partials algorithm.

Name _____ Date _____

Unit 19 Home Practice

PART 1

Tell whether the sum of each is more than 600, less than 600, or equal to 600.

1. 300 + 300 _____ 2. 318 + 264 _____
3. 268 + 295 _____ 4. 329 + 282 _____
5. 240 + 360 _____ 6. 363 + 302 _____

Fill in the blanks below so each number sentence equals 1000.

7. _____ + _____ + 300 = 1000

8. _____ + 150 + _____ = 1000

9. 335 + _____ + _____ = 1000

PART 2

1.	2.	3.	4.	5.	6.
79 + 69	979 − 430	75 × 4	32 × 9	60 × 4	83 × 7

7. Find two 3-digit numbers whose sum is 251. _____

_____

8. Find two numbers whose difference is 79. _____

_____

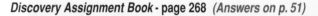

268 DAB • Grade 3 • Unit 19   MULTIPLICATION AND DIVISION PROBLEMS

Discovery Assignment Book **- page 268** *(Answers on p. 51)*

At a Glance

Math Facts and Daily Practice and Problems

DPP Bit E and Task H provide practice with the last six multiplication facts. Items C, D, F, G, and I provide computation practice. Task J asks students to compare rectangles and squares.

Part 1. Writing Multiplication Stories

1. Write a one-digit by one-digit multiplication problem on the board, such as 4 × 8.
2. Students write and illustrate a story to represent it.
3. Write a one-digit by two-digit problem on the board, such as 4 × 26.
4. Students write stories, illustrate their stories, and solve the problems using their own methods.
5. Students explain their methods to the class.

Part 2. Break-apart Products and Their Matching Stories

1. Students read Peter's story and solution to 4 × 26 on the *More Multiplication Stories* Activity Pages in the *Student Guide.*
2. Point out that Peter revised his story to reflect the way he broke apart the numbers in his solution.
3. Provide another example showing how to revise a story to match a partition used in a solution.
4. Choose a few solutions involving breaking numbers apart that the class wrote for 4 × 26.
5. The class helps to revise the stories so they match the way the numbers were broken apart.

Part 3. Breaking Factors into Tens and Ones

1. Focus on breaking apart products by partitioning factors into tens and ones.
2. Read and discuss Libby's and Alex's stories on the *More Multiplication Stories* Activity Pages.
3. Students write and illustrate stories for two-digit multiplication problems, as a class and individually.
4. Students use pictures to solve the problems. They create number sentences for their pictures.
5. In the Solving Problems Tyrone's Way section in the *Student Guide,* students solve two-digit by one-digit multiplication problems. Students divide their solutions into four parts: products to add, calculations, story, and picture. *(Questions 1–8)*

Part 4. An Algorithm for Multiplication (Maria's Way)

1. Introduce the multiplication algorithm shown in the Solving Problems Maria's Way section in the *Student Guide.*
2. Students practice using this algorithm in *Questions 9–16.*
3. Encourage students to check whether their answers are reasonable.

Homework

1. Assign Home Practice Part 2.
2. Assign the Homework section in the *Student Guide.*

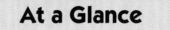

At a Glance

1. Ask students to solve the problem 4 × 34 representing their work Tyrone's Way. Record your observations using the *Observational Assessment Record.*
2. Use the homework problems in the *Student Guide* to assess students' understanding of the paper-and-pencil algorithm.

Connection

1. Students can use *Kid Pix* to illustrate their stories.
2. Use *The National Library of Virtual Manipulatives* website to work with manipulatives to model the all-partials algorithm.

Answer Key is on pages 50–51.

Notes:

Solve the following problems by first breaking the two-digit number into tens and ones and then multiplying. For each problem, write a story, and draw pictures to match your solution. Organize your work the way Tyrone organized his. You may use your multiplication tables to help you with any facts you need.

1. $3 \times 54 = ?$ 2. $31 \times 8 = ?$

3. $5 \times 67 = ?$ 4. $45 \times 6 = ?$

5. $4 \times 28 = ?$ 6. $62 \times 5 = ?$

7. $58 \times 5 = ?$ 8. $7 \times 36 = ?$

Solving Problems Maria's Way

Maria recorded her work like this:

$$37 \quad \rightarrow \quad 30 + 7 \quad \text{step 1}$$
$$\times 4$$
$$28 \quad \leftarrow \quad 4 \times 7 \quad \text{step 2}$$
$$+ 120 \quad \leftarrow \quad 4 \times 30 \quad \text{step 3}$$
$$148 \quad \quad \text{answer}$$

Solve the following problems, showing your work as Maria did.

9. $21 \times 8 = ?$ 10. $84 \times 3 = ?$

11. $75 \times 3 = ?$ 12. $61 \times 5 = ?$

13. $46 \times 8 = ?$ 14. $52 \times 9 = ?$

15. $34 \times 6 = ?$ 16. $91 \times 5 = ?$

Homework

Solve the following problems, showing your work as either Tyrone or Maria did.

1. $2 \times 87 = ?$ 2. $23 \times 9 = ?$ 3. $9 \times 13 = ?$

4. $34 \times 9 = ?$ 5. $4 \times 79 = ?$ 6. $18 \times 7 = ?$

7. $6 \times 68 = ?$ 8. $53 \times 8 = ?$ 9. $42 \times 5 = ?$

10. Solve 3×37. Write a story, and draw a picture to match your solution.

294   SG • Grade 3 • Unit 19 • Lesson 2   More Multiplication Stories

Student Guide - page 294

Student Guide (p. 294)

Stories and pictures will vary.

1. 3×54
$$3 \times 50 = 150$$
$$3 \times 4 = 12$$
$$3 \times 54 = 150 + 12 = 162$$

2. 31×8
$$30 \times 8 = 240$$
$$1 \times 8 = 8$$
$$31 \times 8 = 240 + 8 = 248$$

3. 5×67
$$5 \times 60 = 300$$
$$5 \times 7 = 35$$
$$5 \times 67 = 300 + 35 = 335$$

4. 45×6
$$40 \times 6 = 240$$
$$5 \times 6 = 30$$
$$45 \times 6 = 240 + 30 = 270$$

5. 4×28
$$4 \times 20 = 80$$
$$4 \times 8 = 32$$
$$4 \times 28 = 80 + 32 = 112$$

6. 62×5
$$60 \times 5 = 300$$
$$2 \times 5 = 10$$
$$62 \times 5 = 300 + 10 = 310$$

7. 58×5
$$50 \times 5 = 250$$
$$8 \times 5 = 40$$
$$58 \times 5 = 250 + 40 = 290$$

8. 7×36
$$7 \times 30 = 210$$
$$7 \times 6 = 42$$
$$7 \times 36 = 210 + 42 = 252$$

9.
$$\begin{array}{r} 21 \\ \times\ 8 \\ \hline 8 \\ +\ 160 \\ \hline 168 \end{array}$$

10.
$$\begin{array}{r} 84 \\ \times\ 3 \\ \hline 12 \\ +\ 240 \\ \hline 252 \end{array}$$

11.
$$\begin{array}{r} 75 \\ \times\ 3 \\ \hline 15 \\ +\ 210 \\ \hline 225 \end{array}$$

12.
$$\begin{array}{r} 61 \\ \times\ 5 \\ \hline 5 \\ +\ 300 \\ \hline 305 \end{array}$$

13.
$$\begin{array}{r} 46 \\ \times\ 8 \\ \hline 48 \\ +\ 320 \\ \hline 368 \end{array}$$

14.
$$\begin{array}{r} 52 \\ \times\ 9 \\ \hline 18 \\ +\ 450 \\ \hline 468 \end{array}$$

15.
$$\begin{array}{r} 34 \\ \times\ 6 \\ \hline 24 \\ +\ 180 \\ \hline 204 \end{array}$$

16.
$$\begin{array}{r} 91 \\ \times\ 5 \\ \hline 5 \\ +\ 450 \\ \hline 455 \end{array}$$

Homework

1. 174   2. 207
3. 117   4. 306
5. 316   6. 126
7. 408   8. 424
9. 210   10. 111; stories and pictures will vary.

Discovery Assignment Book (p. 268)

Home Practice*

Part 2

1. 148   2. 549
3. 300   4. 288
5. 240   6. 581
7. Answers will vary. One example is
   111 + 140 = 251
8. Answers will vary. One example is
   164 − 85 = 79

Name _____ Date _____

Unit 19 **Home Practice**

PART 1

Tell whether the sum of each is more than 600, less than 600, or equal to 600.

1. 300 + 300 _____   2. 318 + 264 _____
3. 268 + 295 _____   4. 329 + 282 _____
5. 240 + 360 _____   6. 363 + 302 _____

Fill in the blanks below so each number sentence equals 1000.

7. ____ + ____ + 300 = 1000
8. ____ + 150 + ____ = 1000
9. 335 + ____ + ____ = 1000

PART 2

1.	2.	3.	4.	5.	6.
79	979	75	32	60	83
+ 69	− 430	× 4	× 9	× 4	× 7

7. Find two 3-digit numbers whose sum is 251. _____
   _____

8. Find two numbers whose difference is 79. _____
   _____

268 DAB · Grade 3 · Unit 19   MULTIPLICATION AND DIVISION PROBLEMS

Discovery Assignment Book - page 268

---

*Answers for all the Home Practice in the *Discovery Assignment Book* are at the end of the unit.

Lesson 3

Making Groups

Lesson Overview

Students consider the number of groups of equal size they can make from various numbers of objects. The groupings involve dividing numbers between 25 and 50, many of which cannot be solved using a simple reversal of multiplication facts. Particular attention is given to remainders.

Key Content

- Dividing a set of objects into equal-size groups (with remainders).
- Representing division problems using drawings and manipulatives.
- Writing number sentences for division situations.
- Dividing two-digit numbers.
- Investigating patterns involving remainders.
- Interpreting remainders.

Math Facts

DPP Bit K provides practice with using doubles to solve multiplication problems.

Homework

1. Assign Home Practice Part 3.
2. Ask students to complete a table for 56 like the one they completed in the lesson.

Assessment

1. While students complete a table like the one in the lesson, observe their abilities to write number sentences for division situations and interpret remainders. Record observations on the *Observational Assessment Record*.
2. Use DPP Task L as an assessment.

Curriculum Sequence

Making Groups

Students divided objects into equal-size groups with remainders in Grade 3 Unit 3 Lesson 4 *Making Groups*.

Materials List

Supplies and Copies

Student	Teacher
Supplies for Each Student • 50 connecting cubes	**Supplies**
Copies • 4–5 copies of *Four-column Data Table* per student (*Unit Resource Guide* Page 58)	**Copies/Transparencies**

All blackline masters including assessment, transparency, and DPP masters are also on the Teacher Resource CD.

Daily Practice and Problems and Home Practice

DPP items K–L (*Unit Resource Guide* Pages 19–20)
Home Practice Part 3 (*Discovery Assignment Book* Page 296)

Note: Classrooms whose pacing differs significantly from the suggested pacing of the units should use the Math Facts Calendar in Section 4 of the *Facts Resource Guide* to ensure students receive the complete math facts program.

Assessment Tools

Observational Assessment Record (*Unit Resource Guide* Pages 11–12)

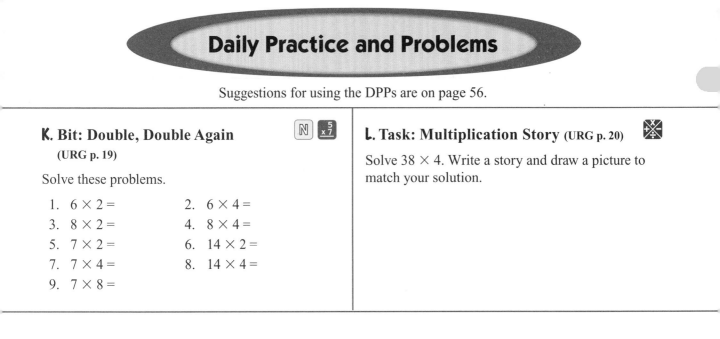

Daily Practice and Problems

Suggestions for using the DPPs are on page 56.

K. Bit: Double, Double Again
   (URG p. 19)

Solve these problems.

1. 6 × 2 =
2. 6 × 4 =
3. 8 × 2 =
4. 8 × 4 =
5. 7 × 2 =
6. 14 × 2 =
7. 7 × 4 =
8. 14 × 4 =
9. 7 × 8 =

L. Task: Multiplication Story (URG p. 20)

Solve 38 × 4. Write a story and draw a picture to match your solution.

This activity is similar to the activity *Making Groups* from Unit 3 *Exploring Multiplication.* However, this activity involves larger numbers and emphasizes division rather than multiplication.

On the board, write a number between 25 and 50. This will represent the number of objects to be divided into groups. (In the following discussion, 30 is used as an example.) Ask students to suggest a number to represent the size of the groups to be made. (We will use 7 as an example.) Ask the class how many groups of that size can be made from the objects and how many will be left over.

To help them think about the problem, students can divide collections of connecting cubes into groups or they can write Xs in rows to represent groups of objects. For example, if the number of objects is 30 and the number in each group is 7, they can write 4 rows of 7 Xs, with 2 left over:

$$
\begin{array}{l}
\text{X X X X X X X} \\
\text{X X X X X X X} \\
\text{X X X X X X X} \\
\text{X X X X X X X} \\
\text{X X} \qquad\qquad 30 \div 7 = 4\ \text{R2}
\end{array}
$$

Ask for another number for the size of a group. Tell students to find out how many groups they can now make using the new group size. Continue in this manner, investigating several different group sizes. Ask students to record their findings on the *Four-column Data Table* or in a similar one they draw on their own paper. They should record the number of objects to be divided into groups at the top of the table. After a discussion of several groupings of 30 objects, their tables should look like Figure 5.

The number to be divided into groups is 30.

Size of Groups	Number of Groups	Number left Over	Number Sentence
7	4	2	$30 \div 7 = 4\ \text{R2}$
2	15	0	$30 \div 2 = 15$
13	2	4	$30 \div 13 = 2\ \text{R4}$
8	3	6	$30 \div 8 = 3\ \text{R6}$
20	1	10	$30 \div 20 = 1\ \text{R10}$

Figure 5: *A sample data table for groupings of 30 objects*

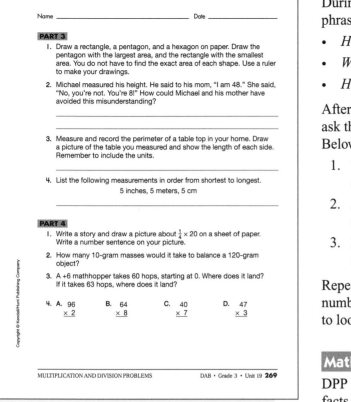

Name _____ Date _____

PART 3

1. Draw a rectangle, a pentagon, and a hexagon on paper. Draw the pentagon with the largest area, and the rectangle with the smallest area. You do not have to find the exact area of each shape. Use a ruler to make your drawings.

2. Michael measured his height. He said to his mom, "I am 48." She said, "No, you're not. You're 8!" How could Michael and his mother have avoided this misunderstanding?

    _____

3. Measure and record the perimeter of a table top in your home. Draw a picture of the table you measured and show the length of each side. Remember to include the units.

4. List the following measurements in order from shortest to longest.
    5 inches, 5 meters, 5 cm

    _____

PART 4

1. Write a story and draw a picture about $\frac{1}{4} \times 20$ on a sheet of paper. Write a number sentence on your picture.

2. How many 10-gram masses would it take to balance a 120-gram object?

3. A +6 mathhopper takes 60 hops, starting at 0. Where does it land? If it takes 63 hops, where does it land?

4. A. 96   B. 64   C. 40   D. 47
        × 2   × 8   × 7   × 3

MULTIPLICATION AND DIVISION PROBLEMS   DAB • Grade 3 • Unit 19 **269**

Discovery Assignment Book **- page 269** *(Answers on p. 59)*

During your discussion, use the various ways to phrase division questions:

- *How many 7s are in 30?*
- *What is 30 divided by 7?*
- *How many times does 7 go into 30?*

After students consider several different group sizes, ask them to write down any patterns they find. Below are some possible responses:

1. The number left over is always less than the size of the group.
2. As you make the group size bigger, the number of groups gets smaller.
3. If the group size is more than half the number of objects, you will have only one group.

Repeat this activity several times with different numbers of objects and ask students to continue to look for patterns.

Math Facts

DPP Bit K provides practice with multiplication facts and using doubles.

Homework and Practice

- Ask students to complete a table for 56 like the one they did in the lesson. Ask students to divide this number into various size groups using a *Four-column Data Table.*
- Home Practice Part 3 asks students to review measuring and finding area and perimeter of different two-dimensional shapes.

Answers for Part 3 of the Home Practice are in the Answer Key at the end of this lesson and at the end of this unit.

Assessment

- Ask students to complete a table like the one they did in the activity for a different number between 20 and 50. Observe students' abilities to write number sentences for division situations and interpret remainders. Record your observations on the *Observational Assessment Record.*
- Use DPP Task L Multiplication Story as an assessment.

Estimated
Class Sessions

1

At a Glance

Math Facts and Daily Practice and Problems

DPP Bit K provides practice with using doubles to solve multiplication problems. Task L asks students to create a story and draw a picture for a multiplication problem.

Teaching the Activity

1. On the board, write a number between 25 and 50 to represent the quantity of cubes to be divided.
2. Students decide how many they want in each group.
3. Students find how many groups and how many remain using cubes or drawings.
4. Students repeat the divisions with other group sizes and record the results and the division number sentences on a *Four-column Data Table.*
5. Students look for patterns in their tables.
6. Students repeat the activity with other group sizes.

Homework

1. Assign Home Practice Part 3.
2. Ask students to complete a table for 56 like the one they completed in the lesson.

Assessment

1. While students complete a table like the one in the lesson, observe their abilities to write number sentences for division situations and interpret remainders. Record observations on the *Observational Assessment Record.*
2. Use DPP Task L as an assessment.

Answer Key is on page 59.

Notes:

Name _____ Date _____

_____

Four-column Data Table, Blackline Master

Discovery Assignment Book (p. 269)

Home Practice*

Part 3

1. Check for size relationship as follows:

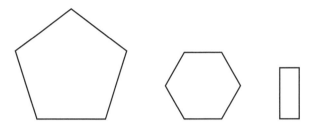

The pentagon and hexagon do not have to be regular shapes. Their sides and angles may vary in size.

2. Answers will vary. However, students' explanations should include the idea that Michael and his mother are confused because neither of them remembered to give the proper unit of measurement. Michael should have said he was 48 inches tall and his mother should have said he was 8 years old.

3. Accept any reasonable answer. The total measurement should equal the sum of the sides. Lengths should be given in inches or centimeters.

4. 5 cm, 5 inches, 5 meters

Name _____ Date _____

PART 3

1. Draw a rectangle, a pentagon, and a hexagon on paper. Draw the pentagon with the largest area, and the rectangle with the smallest area. You do not have to find the exact area of each shape. Use a ruler to make your drawings.

2. Michael measured his height. He said to his mom, "I am 48." She said, "No, you're not. You're 8!" How could Michael and his mother have avoided this misunderstanding?

_____

3. Measure and record the perimeter of a table top in your home. Draw a picture of the table you measured and show the length of each side. Remember to include the units.

_____

4. List the following measurements in order from shortest to longest.
5 inches, 5 meters, 5 cm

_____

PART 4

1. Write a story and draw a picture about $\frac{1}{4} \times 20$ on a sheet of paper. Write a number sentence on your picture.

2. How many 10-gram masses would it take to balance a 120-gram object?

3. A +6 mathhopper takes 60 hops, starting at 0. Where does it land? If it takes 63 hops, where does it land?

4. A. 96   B. 64   C. 40   D. 47
       × 2   × 8   × 7   × 3

MULTIPLICATION AND DIVISION PROBLEMS   DAB • Grade 3 • Unit 19 **269**

Discovery Assignment Book - page 269

---

*Answers for all the Home Practice in the *Discovery Assignment Book* are at the end of the unit.

Lesson 4

Solving Problems with Division

Lesson Overview

Students solve multiplication and division word problems, including some division problems that involve remainders. They also solve challenging multistep problems whose solutions use both multiplication and division.

Key Content

- Solving multiplication and division problems and explaining the reasoning.
- Interpreting remainders.
- Solving multistep word problems.

Math Facts

DPP items P and Q provide practice with and assess multiplication facts.

Homework

1. Assign Home Practice Part 4.
2. Assign the homework problems on the *Solving Problems with Division* Activity Pages.

Assessment

1. DPP Bit Q is a quiz on the last six multiplication facts.
2. Assign the *Multiplication and Division* Assessment Blackline Master. Have multiplication tables available for students.
3. Note students' progress solving multiplication and division problems. Transfer appropriate Unit 19 *Observational Assessment Record* observations to students' *Individual Assessment Record Sheets*.

Curriculum Sequence

Division with Remainders

In Grade 3 Unit 7 Lesson 4 *Birthday Party* and Lesson 5 *Money Jar,* students solved division problems and wrote number sentences for their solutions.

They interpreted remainders, including those resulting from division using a calculator. In Unit 11 Lesson 6 *Division in Lizardland,* students solved word problems involving division and investigated division involving zero.

Materials List

Supplies and Copies

Student	Teacher
Supplies for Each Student • base-ten pieces, optional • connecting cubes, optional • calculators, optional	**Supplies**
Copies • 1 table from *Small Multiplication Tables* per student (*Unit Resource Guide* Page 32) • 1 copy of *Multiplication and Division* per student (*Unit Resource Guide* Page 67)	**Copies/Transparencies**

All blackline masters including assessment, transparency, and DPP masters are also on the Teacher Resource CD.

Student Books
Solving Problems with Division (*Student Guide* Pages 295–298)

Daily Practice and Problems and Home Practice
DPP items M–R (*Unit Resource Guide* Pages 20–22)
Home Practice Part 4 (*Discovery Assignment Book* Page 269)

Note: Classrooms whose pacing differs significantly from the suggested pacing of the units should use the Math Facts Calendar in Section 4 of the *Facts Resource Guide* to ensure students receive the complete math facts program.

Assessment Tools
Observational Assessment Record (*Unit Resource Guide* Pages 11–12)
Individual Assessment Record Sheet (*Teacher Implementation Guide,* Assessment section)

Daily Practice and Problems

Suggestions for using the DPPs are on pages 64–65.

M. Bit: Today, Tonight, or Tomorrow?
(URG p. 20)

1. What time will it be 4 hours from now?
2. What time will it be $6\frac{1}{3}$ hours from now?
3. What time will it be 8 hours from now?
4. What time will it be $12\frac{1}{4}$ hours from now?

P. Task: Rectangles and Products (URG p. 21)

1. Using *Centimeter Grid Paper,* draw all the rectangles you can make with 32 tiles.
2. Draw all the rectangles you can make with 24 tiles.

N. Challenge: Mathhoppers on the Calculator (URG p. 20)

1. A + 9 mathhopper starts at 2 and hops 15 times. Estimate where it lands.
2. Where does it land exactly? Tell how you know.
3. How many more hops does it need to reach 200?

Q. Bit: Multiplication Quiz: The Last Six Facts (URG p. 21)

A. $8 \times 6 =$ B. $6 \times 4 =$
C. $4 \times 7 =$ D. $7 \times 8 =$
E. $6 \times 7 =$ F. $8 \times 4 =$

O. Bit: Some More Sums (URG p. 21)

Add 27 to each of these numbers.

65   189   2977

R. Task: Saturday at Lizardland (URG p. 22)

Use the Lizardland picture from Unit 11 in your *Student Guide* to solve the following problems.

1. On Saturday, in the first hour, 100 adults and 200 children came to Lizardland. How much was collected in ticket sales?
2. Last Saturday 600 adults and 1000 children came to Lizardland. How much was collected in ticket sales?
3. Fifty-nine members of the Jones family reunion came to Lizardland on Saturday. Forty-four family members were children. Fifteen were adults. How much did they pay to get in?

Ask students to solve *Questions 1–7* on the *Solving Problems with Division* Activity Pages. Some are multiplication problems and some are division problems. Many of the division problems involve three-digit dividends. Students can use any method that makes sense to them to solve these problems. No formal division algorithm is introduced at this time.

Students can solve the problems in a variety of ways. Encourage them to share their strategies. Students may:

• Use repeated addition or subtraction to find a solution.

• Use connecting cubes or base-ten pieces to model the process.

• Write a number sentence and use a calculator.

• Estimate a solution and then try a variety of ways to find it.

Discuss students' strategies and encourage them to brainstorm other ways that they might have solved the problems. Encourage students to try a variety of strategies for each problem. Trying multiple strategies will verify their solutions while helping them prepare for later problem-solving situations.

Questions 8–12 are division problems with remainders. The class should discuss the different ways that remainders are treated. In *Question 8*, division gives $250 \div 60 = 4\ R10$. Since the remainder 10 represents the number of children left after four buses are filled and since these children still need to ride a bus, the answer should be rounded up to the next whole number of buses: 5. In *Question 9*, division gives $\$1.00 \div \$.30 = 3\ R\$.10$; the remainder $\$.10$ is extra money. Since it is not enough to buy a pencil, it must be dropped (or put back into Julia's pocket). In *Question 10*, division gives $21 \div 4 = 5\ R1$. The remainder 1 is an extra pizza. It can be cut into fourths so that each class gets one-fourth. Thus, the answer is $5\frac{1}{4}$ pizzas. *Question 11* asks students to divide 23 students into four groups. $23 \div 4 = 5\ R3$. The three remaining students are added to three groups, so that there are three groups of six students and only one group of five students. These problems give different ways to deal with remainders: round up, round down, express as a fraction, and distribute the leftovers as equally as possible.

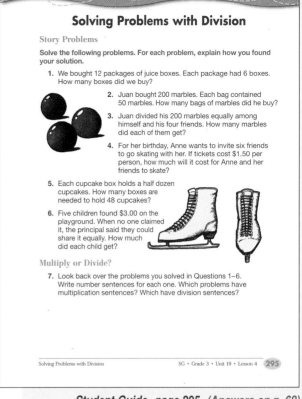

Student Guide - page 295 (*Answers on p. 68*)

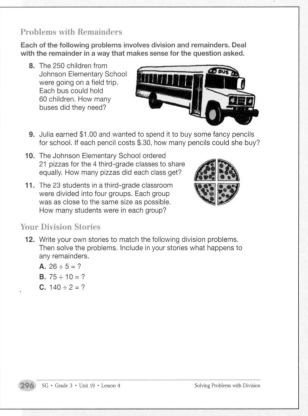

Student Guide - page 296 (*Answers on p. 68*)

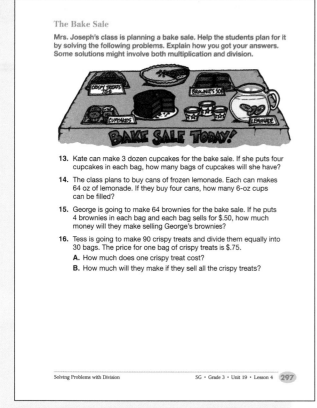

The Bake Sale

Mrs. Joseph's class is planning a bake sale. Help the students plan for it by solving the following problems. Explain how you got your answers. Some solutions might involve both multiplication and division.

13. Kate can make 3 dozen cupcakes for the bake sale. If she puts four cupcakes in each bag, how many bags of cupcakes will she have?

14. The class plans to buy cans of frozen lemonade. Each can makes 64 oz of lemonade. If they buy four cans, how many 6-oz cups can be filled?

15. George is going to make 64 brownies for the bake sale. If he puts 4 brownies in each bag and each bag sells for $.50, how much money will they make selling George's brownies?

16. Tess is going to make 90 crispy treats and divide them equally into 30 bags. The price for one bag of crispy treats is $.75.
   A. How much does one crispy treat cost?
   B. How much will they make if they sell all the crispy treats?

Student Guide - page 297 *(Answers on p. 69)*

Questions 13–16 are more challenging because they require more than one step.

Math Facts

Task P uses rectangles to practice multiplication facts.

Homework and Practice

- DPP Bit M provides practice with time. Challenge N asks students to solve problems using skip counting or multiplication. Bit O provides addition practice. Task R asks students to solve Lizardland problems involving money.

- Assign the Homework section in the *Student Guide.*

- Home Practice Part 4 asks students to solve problems involving multiplication.

Answers for Part 4 of the Home Practice are in the Answer Key at the end of this lesson and at the end of this unit.

Homework

Solve the following problems.

1. $2 \times 8 = ?$
2. $9/3 = ?$
3. $6 \times 7 = ?$
4. $30 \div 5 = ?$
5. $28/4 = ?$
6. $7 \times 9 = ?$
7. $45 \div 5 = ?$
8. $24/6 = ?$
9. $64/8 = ?$
10. $13/1 = ?$
11. $10/2 = ?$
12. $3 \times 7 = ?$

13. A. Elly made one dozen sandwiches for a picnic with 3 of her friends. If the four girls want to share equally, how many sandwiches will each friend get?
   B. Elly's friend Emma brought a 64 oz pitcher of juice to share with the group. How much juice will each friend get?
   C. Elizabeth made 6 cupcakes to share with the group. How many cupcakes will each friend get?

14. Write a story problem to go with one of the multiplication problems in Questions 1–12.

15. Write a story problem to go with one of the division problems in Questions 1–12.

Student Guide - page 298 *(Answers on p. 69)*

Name _____ Date _____

PART 3

1. Draw a rectangle, a pentagon, and a hexagon on paper. Draw the pentagon with the largest area, and the rectangle with the smallest area. You do not have to find the exact area of each shape. Use a ruler to make your drawings.

2. Michael measured his height. He said to his mom, "I am 48." She said, "No, you're not. You're 8!" How could Michael and his mother have avoided this misunderstanding?

_____

3. Measure and record the perimeter of a table top in your home. Draw a picture of the table you measured and show the length of each side. Remember to include the units.

4. List the following measurements in order from shortest to longest.
   5 inches, 5 meters, 5 cm

_____

PART 4

1. Write a story and draw a picture about $\frac{1}{4} \times 20$ on a sheet of paper. Write a number sentence on your picture.

2. How many 10-gram masses would it take to balance a 120-gram object?

3. A +6 mathhopper takes 60 hops, starting at 0. Where does it land? If it takes 63 hops, where does it land?

4. A. $\begin{array}{r} 96 \\ \times\ 2 \end{array}$ B. $\begin{array}{r} 64 \\ \times\ 8 \end{array}$ C. $\begin{array}{r} 40 \\ \times\ 7 \end{array}$ D. $\begin{array}{r} 47 \\ \times\ 3 \end{array}$

Discovery Assignment Book - page 269 *(Answers on p. 70)*

Assessment

- DPP Bit Q is a quiz on the last six multiplication facts.

- Use the *Multiplication and Division* Assessment Blackline Master to assess students' abilities to multiply two-digit by one-digit numbers to solve problems involving multiplication and division. Allow students to use multiplication tables.

- Note students' abilities to solve multiplication and division problems and explain their reasoning on the *Observational Assessment Record*.

- Transfer appropriate Unit 19 observations to students' *Individual Assessment Record Sheets*.

Extension

Use your calendars from the *Multiples on the Calendar* activity to write division sentences. Students can chart the factors and the remainders for certain numbers. Encourage students to look for and discuss patterns in their calendars. Students may recognize that there is a relationship between multiplication and division sentences.

At a Glance

Math Facts and Daily Practice and Problems

DPP Bit M provides practice with time. Items N, O, and R provide computation practice. Items P and Q provide practice with and assess multiplication facts.

Teaching the Activity

1. Students solve *Questions 1–7* on the *Solving Problems with Division* Activity Pages in the *Student Guide* using a variety of strategies. These problems involve multiplication and division.
2. Students brainstorm and discuss other ways to solve these problems.
3. Students solve *Questions 8–12* which involve division and remainders.
4. Students discuss what to do with the remainders in *Questions 8–11.*
5. Students solve *Questions 13–16* which involve more than one step.

Homework

1. Assign Home Practice Part 4.
2. Assign the homework problems on the *Solving Problems with Division* Activity Pages.

Assessment

1. DPP Bit Q is a quiz on the last six multiplication facts.
2. Assign the *Multiplication and Division* Assessment Blackline Master. Have multiplication tables available for students.
3. Note students' progress solving multiplication and division problems. Transfer appropriate Unit 19 *Observational Assessment Record* observations to students' *Individual Assessment Record Sheets.*

Extension

Use your calendars to write division sentences. Students can chart the factors and remainders. Have students identify patterns.

Answer Key is on pages 68–70.

Notes:

Name ______________________ Date ______________

Multiplication and Division

1. Solve 28×3. Write a story and draw a picture to match your solution.

Solve the problems.

2. $\begin{array}{r} 15 \\ \times\ 7 \\ \hline \end{array}$

3. $\begin{array}{r} 30 \\ \times\ 6 \\ \hline \end{array}$

4. $\begin{array}{r} 42 \\ \times\ 9 \\ \hline \end{array}$

5. Four people can ride in each car on the roller coaster in Lizardland. How many cars will it take so that all 26 students from Mr. Carter's third grade can ride the roller coaster? Explain your reasoning.

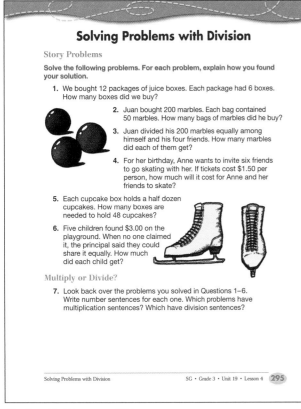

Student Guide - page 295

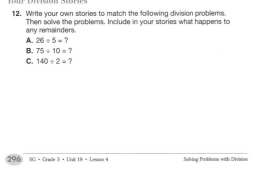

Student Guide - page 296

Student Guide (p. 295)

Solving Problems with Division

Solution strategies will vary.

1. $12 \times 6 = 72$ boxes
2. $200 \div 50 = 4$ bags
3. $200 \div 5 = 40$ marbles
4. $\$1.50 \times 7 = \$10.50$
5. $48 \div 6 = 8$ boxes
6. $\$3.00 \div 5 = \$.60$
7. Answers may vary. For example, in Question 2, students could write either $50 \times 4 = 200$ or $200 \div 50 = 4$.

Student Guide (p. 296)

8. 5 buses*
9. 3 pencils*
10. $5\frac{1}{4}$ pizzas*
11. Three groups had six students and one group had five students.*
12. Answers will vary according to the stories written.

   Check to see that students treat the remainders in ways that match their stories.

*Answers and/or discussion are included in the Lesson Guide.

Student Guide (p. 297)

For *Questions 13–16* solution strategies will vary.

13. 9 bags

14. 42 R4; 42 cups

15. $8.00

16. **A.** $.25

  B. $22.50

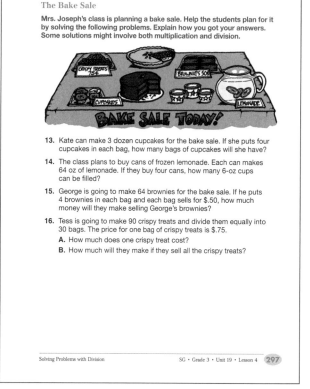

The Bake Sale

Mrs. Joseph's class is planning a bake sale. Help the students plan for it by solving the following problems. Explain how you got your answers. Some solutions might involve both multiplication and division.

13. Kate can make 3 dozen cupcakes for the bake sale. If she puts four cupcakes in each bag, how many bags of cupcakes will she have?

14. The class plans to buy cans of frozen lemonade. Each can makes 64 oz of lemonade. If they buy four cans, how many 6-oz cups can be filled?

15. George is going to make 64 brownies for the bake sale. If he puts 4 brownies in each bag and each bag sells for $.50, how much money will they make selling George's brownies?

16. Tess is going to make 90 crispy treats and divide them equally into 30 bags. The price for one bag of crispy treats is $.75.
  A. How much does one crispy treat cost?
  B. How much will they make if they sell all the crispy treats?

Solving Problems with Division   SG • Grade 3 • Unit 19 • Lesson 4   297

Student Guide - page 297

Student Guide (p. 298)

Homework

1. 16	2. 3
3. 42	4. 6
5. 7	6. 63
7. 9	8. 4
9. 8	10. 13
11. 5	12. 21

13. **A.** $12 \div 4 = 3$ sandwiches per person

  B. $64 \div 4 = 16$ oz of juice per person

  C. $6 \div 4 = 1\frac{1}{2}$ cupcakes per person each or 1 cupcake each and 2 left over

14. Answers will vary.

15. Answers will vary.

Homework

Solve the following problems.

1. $2 \times 8 = ?$
2. $9/3 = ?$
3. $6 \times 7 = ?$
4. $30 \div 5 = ?$
5. $28/4 = ?$
6. $7 \times 9 = ?$
7. $45 \div 5 = ?$
8. $24/6 = ?$
9. $64/8 = ?$
10. $13/1 = ?$
11. $10/2 = ?$
12. $3 \times 7 = ?$

13. **A.** Elly made one dozen sandwiches for a picnic with 3 of her friends. If the four girls want to share equally, how many sandwiches will each friend get?
  B. Elly's friend Emma brought a 64 oz pitcher of juice to share with the group. How much juice will each friend get?
  C. Elizabeth made 6 cupcakes to share with the group. How many cupcakes will each friend get?

14. Write a story problem to go with one of the multiplication problems in Questions 1–12.

15. Write a story problem to go with one of the division problems in Questions 1–12.

298   SG • Grade 3 • Unit 19 • Lesson 4   Solving Problems with Division

Student Guide - page 298

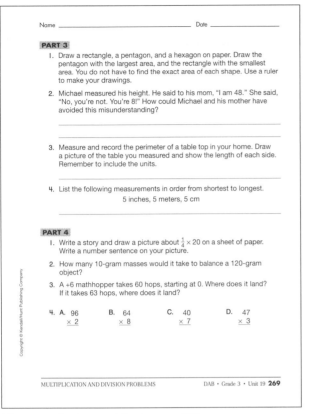

Discovery Assignment Book - page 269

Multiplication and Division

1. Solve 28 × 3. Write a story and draw a picture to match your solution.

Solve the problems.

2. 15
   × 7

3. 30
   × 6

4. 42
   × 9

5. Four people can ride in each car on the roller coaster in Lizardland. How many cars will it take so that all 26 students from Mr. Carter's third grade can ride the roller coaster? Explain your reasoning.

Unit Resource Guide - page 67

Discovery Assignment Book (p. 269)

Home Practice*

Part 4

1. Answers will vary. The story should match the picture. Here is one story and illustration:

    Toni was having a party for twenty people. He knew each person would eat $\frac{1}{4}$ of a super deluxe pizza. How many pizzas does Toni need to order for the party?

$$\frac{1}{4} \times 20 = 5$$

2. 12 10-gram masses

3. 360; 378

4. A. 192

    B. 512

    C. 280

    D. 141

Unit Resource Guide (p. 67)

Multiplication and Division

1. 84; stories and pictures will vary.

2. 105

3. 180

4. 378

5. 26 ÷ 4 = 6 R2; it will take 7 cars for all the students to ride. Six cars will have four students and they need one more car for the two remaining students.

*Answers for all the Home Practice in the *Discovery Assignment Book* are at the end of the unit.

Discovery Assignment Book (p. 268)

Part 1

1. equal

2. less than

3. less than

4. more than

5. equal

6. more than

7. Answers will vary. One example is $400 + 300 + 300 = 1000$

8. Answers will vary. One example is $350 + 150 + 500 = 1000$

9. Answers will vary. One example is $335 + 165 = 500 = 1000$

Part 2

1. 148

2. 549

3. 300

4. 288

5. 240

6. 581

7. Answers will vary. One example is $111 + 140 = 251$

8. Answers will vary. One example is $164 - 85 = 79$

Name _____ Date _____

Unit 19 Home Practice

PART 1

Tell whether the sum of each is more than 600, less than 600, or equal to 600.

1. 300 + 300 _____   2. 318 + 264 _____

3. 268 + 295 _____   4. 329 + 282 _____

5. 240 + 360 _____   6. 363 + 302 _____

Fill in the blanks below so each number sentence equals 1000.

7. _____ + _____ + 300 = 1000

8. _____ + 150 + _____ = 1000

9. 335 + _____ + _____ = 1000

PART 2

1.	2.	3.	4.	5.	6.
79 + 69	979 − 430	75 × 4	32 × 9	60 × 4	83 × 7

7. Find two 3-digit numbers whose sum is 251. _____

_____

8. Find two numbers whose difference is 79. _____

_____

268 DAB • Grade 3 • Unit 19   MULTIPLICATION AND DIVISION PROBLEMS

Discovery Assignment Book - page 268

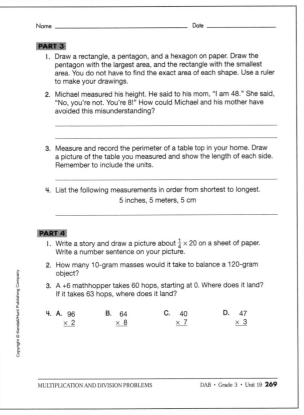

Name _____ Date _____

PART 3

1. Draw a rectangle, a pentagon, and a hexagon on paper. Draw the pentagon with the largest area, and the rectangle with the smallest area. You do not have to find the exact area of each shape. Use a ruler to make your drawings.

2. Michael measured his height. He said to his mom, "I am 48." She said, "No, you're not. You're 8!" How could Michael and his mother have avoided this misunderstanding?

   _____

3. Measure and record the perimeter of a table top in your home. Draw a picture of the table you measured and show the length of each side. Remember to include the units.

   _____

4. List the following measurements in order from shortest to longest.

   5 inches, 5 meters, 5 cm

   _____

PART 4

1. Write a story and draw a picture about $\frac{1}{4} \times 20$ on a sheet of paper. Write a number sentence on your picture.

2. How many 10-gram masses would it take to balance a 120-gram object?

3. A +6 mathhopper takes 60 hops, starting at 0. Where does it land? If it takes 63 hops, where does it land?

4. A. 96   B. 64   C. 40   D. 47
       × 2   × 8   × 7   × 3

MULTIPLICATION AND DIVISION PROBLEMS   DAB • Grade 3 • Unit 19 **269**

Discovery Assignment Book - page 269

Discovery Assignment Book (p. 269)

Part 3

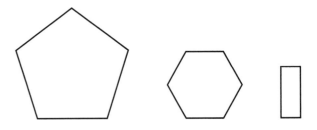

1. Check for size relationship as follows:

   The pentagon and hexagon do not have to be regular shapes. Their sides and angles may vary in size.

2. Answers will vary. However, students' explanations should include the idea that Michael and his mother are confused because neither of them remembered to give the proper unit of measurement. Michael should have said he was 48 inches tall and his mother should have said he was 8 years old.

3. Accept any reasonable answer. The total measurement should equal the sum of the sides. Lengths should be given in inches or centimeters.

4. 5 cm, 5 inches, 5 meters

Part 4

1. Answers will vary. The story should match the picture. Here is one story and illustration:

   Toni was having a party for twenty people. He knew each person would eat $\frac{1}{4}$ of a super deluxe pizza. How many pizzas does Toni need to order for the party?

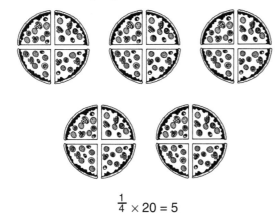

   $$\frac{1}{4} \times 20 = 5$$

2. 12 10-gram masses

3. 360; 378

4. A. 192
   B. 512
   C. 280
   D. 141

Glossary

This glossary provides definitions of key vocabulary terms in the Grade 3 lessons. Locations of key vocabulary terms in the curriculum are included with each definition. Components Key: URG = *Unit Resource Guide*, SG = *Student Guide*, and DAB = *Discovery Assignment Book*.

A

Area (URG Unit 5; SG Unit 5)
The area of a shape is the amount of space it covers, measured in square units.

Array (URG Unit 7 & Unit 11)
An array is an arrangement of elements into a rectangular pattern of (horizontal) rows and (vertical) columns. (*See* column and row.)

Associative Property of Addition (URG Unit 2)
For any three numbers a, b, and c we have $a + (b + c) = (a + b) + c$. For example in finding the sum of 4, 8, and 2, one can compute $4 + 8$ first and then add 2: $(4 + 8) + 2 = 14$. Alternatively, we can compute $8 + 2$ and then add the result to 4: $4 + (8 + 2) = 4 + 10 = 14$.

Average (URG Unit 5)
A number that can be used to represent a typical value in a set of data. (*See also* mean and median.)

Axes (URG Unit 8; SG Unit 8)
Reference lines on a graph. In the Cartesian coordinate system, the axes are two perpendicular lines that meet at the origin. The singular of axes is axis.

B

Base (of a cube model) (URG Unit 18; SG Unit 18)
The part of a cube model that sits on the "ground."

Base-Ten Board (URG Unit 4)
A tool to help children organize base-ten pieces when they are representing numbers.

Base-Ten Pieces (URG Unit 4; SG Unit 4)
A set of manipulatives used to model our number system as shown in the figure at the right. Note that a skinny is made of 10 bits, a flat is made of 100 bits, and a pack is made of 1000 bits.

Base-Ten Shorthand (SG Unit 4)
A pictorial representation of the base-ten pieces as shown.

Nickname	Picture	Shorthand
bit		
skinny		/
flat		
pack		

Best-Fit Line (URG Unit 9; SG Unit 9; DAB Unit 9)
The line that comes closest to the most number of points on a point graph.

Bit (URG Unit 4; SG Unit 4)
A cube that measures 1 cm on each edge. It is the smallest of the base-ten pieces that is often used to represent 1. (*See also* base-ten pieces.)

C

Capacity (URG Unit 16)
1. The volume of the inside of a container.
2. The largest volume a container can hold.

Cartesian Coordinate System (URG Unit 8)
A method of locating points on a flat surface by means of numbers. This method is named after its originator, René Descartes. (*See also* coordinates.)

Centimeter (cm)
A unit of measure in the metric system equal to one-hundredth of a meter. (1 inch = 2.54 cm)

Column (URG Unit 11)
In an array, the objects lined up vertically.

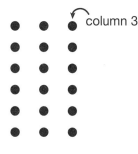
column 3

Common Fraction (URG Unit 15)
Any fraction that is written with a numerator and denominator that are whole numbers. For example, $\frac{3}{4}$ and $\frac{9}{4}$ are both common fractions. (*See also* decimal fraction.)

Commutative Property of Addition (URG Unit 2 & Unit 11)
This is also known as the Order Property of Addition. Changing the order of the addends does not change the sum. For example, $3 + 5 = 5 + 3 = 8$. Using variables, $n + m = m + n$.

Commutative Property of Multiplication (URG Unit 11)
Changing the order of the factors in a multiplication problem does not change the result, e.g., $7 \times 3 = 3 \times 7 = 21$. (*See also* turn-around facts.)

Congruent (URG Unit 12 & Unit 17; SG Unit 12)
Figures with the same shape and size.

Convenient Number (URG Unit 6)
A number used in computation that is close enough to give a good estimate, but is also easy to compute mentally, e.g., 25 and 30 are convenient numbers for 27.

Coordinates (URG Unit 8; SG Unit 8)
An ordered pair of numbers that locates points on a flat surface by giving distances from a pair of coordinate axes. For example, if a point has coordinates (4, 5) it is 4 units from the vertical axis and 5 units from the horizontal axis.

Counting Back (URG Unit 2)
A strategy for subtracting in which students start from a larger number and then count down until the number is reached. For example, to solve $8 - 3$, begin with 8 and count down three, 7, 6, 5.

Counting Down (*See* counting back.)

Counting Up (URG Unit 2)
A strategy for subtraction in which the student starts at the lower number and counts on to the higher number. For example, to solve $8 - 5$, the student starts at 5 and counts up three numbers (6, 7, 8). So $8 - 5 = 3$.

Cube (SG Unit 18)
A three-dimensional shape with six congruent square faces.

Cubic Centimeter (cc) (URG Unit 16; SG Unit 16)
The volume of a cube that is one centimeter long on each edge.

cubic centimeter

Cup (URG Unit 16)
A unit of volume equal to 8 fluid ounces, one-half pint.

D

Decimal Fraction (URG Unit 15)
A fraction written as a decimal. For example, 0.75 and 0.4 are decimal fractions and $\frac{75}{100}$ and $\frac{4}{10}$ are called common fractions. (*See also* fraction.)

Denominator (URG Unit 13)
The number below the line in a fraction. The denominator indicates the number of equal parts in which the unit whole is divided. For example, the 5 is the denominator in the fraction $\frac{2}{5}$. In this case the unit whole is divided into five equal parts.

Density (URG Unit 16)
The ratio of an object's mass to its volume.

Difference (URG Unit 2)
The answer to a subtraction problem.

Dissection (URG Unit 12 & Unit 17)
Cutting or decomposing a geometric shape into smaller shapes that cover it exactly.

Distributive Property of Multiplication over Addition (URG Unit 19)
For any three numbers a, b, and c, $a \times (b + c) = a \times b + a \times c$. The distributive property is the foundation for most methods of multidigit multiplication. For example, $9 \times (17) = 9 \times (10 + 7) = 9 \times 10 + 9 \times 7 = 90 + 63 = 153$.

E

Equal-Arm Balance
See two-pan balance.

Equilateral Triangle (URG Unit 7)
A triangle with all sides of equal length and all angles of equal measure.

Equivalent Fractions (SG Unit 17)
Fractions that have the same value, e.g., $\frac{2}{4} = \frac{1}{2}$.

Estimate (URG Unit 5 & Unit 6)
1. (verb) To find *about* how many.
2. (noun) An approximate number.

Extrapolation (URG Unit 7)
Using patterns in data to make predictions or to estimate values that lie beyond the range of values in the set of data.

F

Fact Family (URG Unit 11; SG Unit 11)
Related math facts, e.g., $3 \times 4 = 12$, $4 \times 3 = 12$, $12 \div 3 = 4$, $12 \div 4 = 3$.

Factor (URG Unit 11; SG Unit 11)
1. In a multiplication problem, the numbers that are multiplied together. In the problem $3 \times 4 = 12$, 3 and 4 are the factors.
2. Whole numbers that can be multiplied together to get a number. That is, numbers that divide a number evenly, e.g., 1, 2, 3, 4, 6, and 12 are all the factors of 12.

Fewest Pieces Rule (URG Unit 4 & Unit 6; SG Unit 4)
Using the least number of base-ten pieces to represent a number. (*See also* base-ten pieces.)

Flat (URG Unit 4; SG Unit 4)
A block that measures 1 cm × 10 cm × 10 cm. It is one of the base-ten pieces that is often used to represent 100. (*See also* base-ten pieces.)

Flip (URG Unit 12)
A motion of the plane in which a figure is reflected over a line so that any point and its image are the same distance from the line.

Fraction (URG Unit 15)
A number that can be written as $\frac{a}{b}$ where a and b are whole numbers and b is not zero. For example, $\frac{1}{2}$, 0.5, and 2 are all fractions since 0.5 can be written as $\frac{5}{10}$ and 2 can be written as $\frac{2}{1}$.

Front-End Estimation (URG Unit 6)
Estimation by looking at the left-most digit.

G

Gallon (gal) (URG Unit 16)
A unit of volume equal to four quarts.

Gram
The basic unit used to measure mass.

H

Hexagon (SG Unit 12)
A six-sided polygon.

Horizontal Axis (SG Unit 1)
In a coordinate grid, the *x*-axis. The axis that extends from left to right.

I

Interpolation (URG Unit 7)
Making predictions or estimating values that lie between data points in a set of data.

J

K

Kilogram
1000 grams.

L

Likely Event (SG Unit 1)
An event that has a high probability of occurring.

Line of Symmetry (URG Unit 12)
A line is a line of symmetry for a plane figure if, when the figure is folded along this line, the two parts match exactly.

Line Symmetry (URG Unit 12; SG Unit 12)
A figure has line symmetry if it has at least one line of symmetry.

Liter (l) (URG Unit 16; SG Unit 16)
Metric unit used to measure volume. A liter is a little more than a quart.

M

Magic Square (URG Unit 2)
A square array of digits in which the sums of the rows, columns, and main diagonals are the same.

Making a Ten (URG Unit 2)
Strategies for addition and subtraction that make use of knowing the sums to ten. For example, knowing $6 + 4 = 10$ can be helpful in finding $10 - 6 = 4$ and $11 - 6 = 5$.

Mass (URG Unit 9 & Unit 16; SG Unit 9)
The amount of matter in an object.

Mean (URG Unit 5)
An average of a set of numbers that is found by adding the values of the data and dividing by the number of values.

Measurement Division (URG Unit 7)
Division as equal grouping. The total number of objects and the number of objects in each group are known. The number of groups is the unknown. For example, tulip bulbs come in packages of 8. If 216 bulbs are sold, how many packages are sold?

Measurement Error (URG Unit 9)
The unavoidable error that occurs due to the limitations inherent to any measurement instrument.

Median (URG Unit 5; DAB Unit 5)
For a set with an odd number of data arranged in order, it is the middle number. For an even number of data arranged in order, it is the number halfway between the two middle numbers.

Meniscus (URG Unit 16; SG Unit 16)
The curved surface formed when a liquid creeps up the side of a container (for example, a graduated cylinder).

Meter (m)
The standard unit of length measure in the metric system. One meter is approximately 39 inches.

Milliliter (ml) (URG Unit 16; SG Unit 16)
A measure of capacity in the metric system that is the volume of a cube that is one centimeter long on each edge.

Multiple (URG Unit 3 & Unit 11)
A number is a multiple of another number if it is evenly divisible by that number. For example, 12 is a multiple of 2 since 2 divides 12 evenly.

N

Numerator (URG Unit 13)
The number written above the line in a fraction. For example, the 2 is the numerator in the fraction $\frac{2}{5}$. (*See also* denominator.)

O

One-Dimensional Object (URG Unit 18; SG Unit 18)
An object is one-dimensional if it is made up of pieces of lines and curves.

Ordered Pairs (URG Unit 8)
A pair of numbers that gives the coordinates of a point on a grid in relation to the origin. The horizontal coordinate is given first; the vertical coordinate is given second. For example, the ordered pair (5, 3) tells us to move five units to the right of the origin and 3 units up.

Origin (URG Unit 8)
The point at which the *x*- and *y*-axes (horizontal and vertical axes) intersect on a coordinate plane. The origin is described by the ordered pair (0, 0) and serves as a reference point so that all the points on the plane can be located by ordered pairs.

P

Pack (URG Unit 4; SG Unit 4)
A cube that measures 10 cm on each edge. It is one of the base-ten pieces that is often used to represent 1000. (*See also* base-ten pieces.)

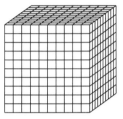

Palindrome (URG Unit 6)
A number, word, or phrase that reads the same forward and backward, e.g., 12321.

Parallel Lines (URG Unit 18)
Lines that are in the same direction. In the plane, parallel lines are lines that do not intersect.

Parallelogram (URG Unit 18)
A quadrilateral with two pairs of parallel sides.

Partitive Division (URG Unit 7)
Division as equal sharing. The total number of objects and the number of groups are known. The number of objects in each group is the unknown. For example, Frank has 144 marbles that he divides equally into 6 groups. How many marbles are in each group?

Pentagon (SG Unit 12)
A five-sided, five-angled polygon.

Perimeter (URG Unit 7; DAB Unit 7)
The distance around a two-dimensional shape.

Pint (URG Unit 16)
A unit of volume measure equal to 16 fluid ounces, i.e., two cups.

Polygon
A two-dimensional connected figure made of line segments in which each endpoint of every side meets with an endpoint of exactly one other side.

Population (URG Unit 1; SG Unit 1)
A collection of persons or things whose properties will be analyzed in a survey or experiment.

Prediction (SG Unit 1)
Using data to declare or foretell what is likely to occur.

Prime Number (URG Unit 11)
A number that has exactly two factors. For example, 7 has exactly two distinct factors, 1 and 7.

Prism
A three-dimensional figure that has two congruent faces, called bases, that are parallel to each other, and all other faces are parallelograms.

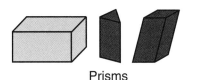

Prisms   Not a prism

Product (URG Unit 11; SG Unit 11; DAB Unit 11)
The answer to a multiplication problem. In the problem $3 \times 4 = 12$, 12 is the product.

Q

Quadrilateral (URG Unit 18)
A polygon with four sides.

Quart (URG Unit 16)
A unit of volume equal to 32 fluid ounces; one quarter of a gallon.

R

Recording Sheet (URG Unit 4)
A place value chart used for addition and subtraction problems.

Rectangular Prism (URG Unit 18; SG Unit 18)
A prism whose bases are rectangles. A right rectangular prism is a prism having all faces rectangles.

Regular (URG Unit 7; DAB Unit 7)
A polygon is regular if all sides are of equal length and all angles are equal.

Remainder (URG Unit 7)
Something that remains or is left after a division problem. The portion of the dividend that is not evenly divisible by the divisor, e.g., $16 \div 5 = 3$ with 1 as a remainder.

Right Angle (SG Unit 12)
An angle that measures 90°.

Rotation (turn) (URG Unit 12)
A transformation (motion) in which a figure is turned a specified angle and direction around a point.

Row (URG Unit 11)
In an array, the objects lined up horizontally.

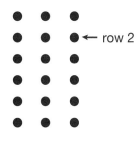

← row 2

Rubric (URG Unit 2)
A written guideline for assigning scores to student work, for the purpose of assessment.

S

Sample (URG Unit 1; SG Unit 1)
A part or subset of a population.

Skinny (URG Unit 4; SG Unit 4)
A block that measures 1 cm $\times$ 1 cm $\times$ 10 cm. It is one of the base-ten pieces that is often used to represent 10. (*See also* base-ten pieces.)

Square Centimeter (sq cm) (SG Unit 5)
The area of a square that is 1 cm long on each side.

Square Number (SG Unit 11)
A number that is the product of a whole number multiplied by itself. For example, 25 is a square number since $5 \times 5 = 25$. A square number can be represented by a square array with the same number of rows as columns. A square array for 25 has 5 rows of 5 objects in each row or 25 total objects.

Standard Masses
A set of objects with convenient masses, usually 1 g, 10 g, 100 g, etc.

Sum (URG Unit 2; SG Unit 2)
The answer to an addition problem.

Survey (URG Unit 14; SG Unit 14)
An investigation conducted by collecting data from a sample of a population and then analyzing it. Usually surveys are used to make predictions about the entire population.

T

Tangrams (SG Unit 12)
A type of geometric puzzle. A shape is given and it must be covered exactly with seven standard shapes called tans.

Thinking Addition (URG Unit 2)
A strategy for subtraction that uses a related addition problem. For example, $15 - 7 = 8$ because $8 + 7 = 15$.

Three-Dimensional (URG Unit 18; SG Unit 18)
Existing in three-dimensional space; having length, width, and depth.

TIMS Laboratory Method (URG Unit 1; SG Unit 1)
A method that students use to organize experiments and investigations. It involves four components: draw, collect, graph, and explore. It is a way to help students learn about the scientific method.

Turn (URG Unit 12)
(*See* rotation.)

Turn-Around Facts (URG Unit 2 & Unit 11 p. 37; SG Unit 11)
Addition facts that have the same addends but in a different order, e.g., $3 + 4 = 7$ and $4 + 3 = 7$. (*See also* commutative property of addition and commutative property of multiplication.)

Two-Dimensional (URG Unit 18; SG Unit 18)
Existing in the plane; having length and width.

Two-Pan Balance
A device for measuring the mass of an object by balancing the object against a number of standard masses (usually multiples of 1 unit, 10 units, and 100 units, etc.).

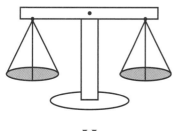

U

Unit (of measurement) (URG Unit 18)
A precisely fixed quantity used to measure. For example, centimeter, foot, kilogram, and quart are units of measurement.

Using a Ten (URG Unit 2)
1. A strategy for addition that uses partitions of the number 10. For example, one can find $8 + 6$ by thinking $8 + 6 = 8 + 2 + 4 = 10 + 4 = 14$.
2. A strategy for subtraction that uses facts that involve subtracting 10. For example, students can use $17 - 10 = 7$ to learn the "close fact" $17 - 9 = 8$.

Using Doubles (URG Unit 2)
Strategies for addition and subtraction that use knowing doubles. For example, one can find $7 + 8$ by thinking $7 + 8 = 7 + 7 + 1 = 14 + 1 = 15$. Knowing $7 + 7 = 14$ can be helpful in finding $14 - 7 = 7$ and $14 - 8 = 6$.

V

Value (URG Unit 1; SG Unit 1)
The possible outcomes of a variable. For example, red, green, and blue are possible values for the variable *color*. Two meters and 1.65 meters are possible values for the variable *length*.

Variable (URG Unit 1; SG Unit 1)
1. An attribute or quantity that changes or varies.
2. A symbol that can stand for a variable.

Vertex (URG Unit 12; SG Unit 12)
1. A point where the sides of a polygon meet.
2. A point where the edges of a three-dimensional object meet.

Vertical Axis (SG Unit 1)
In a coordinate grid, the *y*-axis. It is perpendicular to the horizontal axis.

Volume (URG Unit 16; SG Unit 16)
The measure of the amount of space occupied by an object.

Volume by Displacement (URG Unit 16)
A way of measuring volume of an object by measuring the amount of water (or some other fluid) it displaces.

W

Weight (URG Unit 9)
A measure of the pull of gravity on an object. One unit for measuring weight is the pound.

X

Y

Z